MICAH
FOR YOU

STEPHEN UM

MICAH
FOR YOU

thegoodbook
COMPANY

Micah For You

© Stephen Um/The Good Book Company, 2018.
Reprinted 2021.

Published by:
The Good Book Company

thegoodbook.com | thegoodbook.co.uk
thegoodbook.com.au | thegoodbook.co.nz | thegoodbook.co.in

ISBN: 9781909559745

Design by André Parker

Printed in India

CONTENTS

SERIES PREFACE

Each volume of the *God's Word For You* series takes you to the heart of a book of the Bible, and applies its truths to your heart.

The central aim of each title is to be:

- Bible centered
- Christ glorifying
- Relevantly applied
- Easily readable

You can use *Micah For You:*

To read. You can simply read from cover to cover, as a book that explains and explores the themes, encouragements and challenges of this part of Scripture.

To feed. You can work through this book as part of your own personal regular devotions, or use it alongside a sermon or Bible-study series at your church. Each chapter is divided into two (or occasionally three) shorter sections, with questions for reflection at the end of each.

To lead. You can use this as a resource to help you teach God's word to others, both in small-group and whole-church settings. You'll find tricky verses or concepts explained using ordinary language, and helpful themes and illustrations along with suggested applications.

These books are not commentaries. They assume no understanding of the original Bible languages, nor a high level of biblical knowledge. Verse references are marked in **bold** so that you can refer to them easily. Any words that are used rarely or differently in everyday language outside the church are marked in gray when they first appear, and are explained in a glossary toward the back. There, you'll also find details of resources you can use alongside this one, in both personal and church life.

Our prayer is that as you read, you'll be struck not by the contents of this book, but by the book it's helping you open up; and that you'll praise not the author of this book, but the One he is pointing you to.

Carl Laferton, Series Editor

Bible translations used:

- ESV: English Standard Version (This is the version being quoted unless otherwise stated.)

- NIV: New International Version (2011 edition)

- NIV84: New International Version (1984 edition)

INTRODUCTION TO MICAH

We live in a broken world. But it is not a world beyond hope.

Exploitation tells us that something about this world is off. Oppression tells us that things are not the way they are supposed to be. And when we are honest, our hearts tell us that we are not the way we are supposed to be, or would like to be. We easily choose greed over generosity. We easily choose our comforts over others' needs. Wherever we look, we find something that makes us wonder why our world is the way it is.

These are the moments when we experience our innate longing for justice, mercy, fairness, and goodness. Whenever these desires are met in part, it's as if the world finally seems to be on the right track. It's almost as if the world is upside down, and justice allows us to catch a glimpse of the world right side up. This is why there are so many humanitarian efforts to fight against the constant reminders and the tragic manifestations of this broken and fallen world.

Our longing for justice is not just a 21st-century reality. It's a human reality. Ancient people have always been, and modern people still are, exploring the ideas of fairness, mercy, and goodness. What should these look like? How do we experience them? How do we pursue them? What prevents us from experiencing these realities in every moment we are awake?

Micah—this Old Testament prophet sent to speak God's word to God's people in the 8th century BC—deals with these tough questions. He speaks to us and our world as much as he spoke to his own. The most famous verse from Micah comes from chapter 6: "He has told you, O man, what is good; and what does the Lord require of you but to do justice, and to love kindness, and to walk humbly with your God?" (6:6). You may have seen this verse on a poster or a bumper sticker. Micah 6:6 seems to succinctly summarize the heart of Micah, and it resonates with our desires to see goodness all around us. But when we take the time to read the entire book of Micah carefully, we realize that God is not simply giving us a homework assignment about justice. The message for us is not simply a call to action to do good. God wants us to know the reason and the need for doing good—for his glory and for the flourishing of his creation—and to find the power to do it. Micah tells us that the sin of injustice is real, and that judgment is inevitable, but hope of restoration is coming. God has so much more to say to us through Micah than we might think.

As we walk through Micah, again and again we will see these major themes:

- *Sin.* Micah does not shy away from giving the word of God that lost people in the world of self-gain desperately need to hear. What the Israelites needed was a sobering exposure to the destructive nature of sin and God's absolute abhorrence of injustice. God is disgusted by oppression and abuse. He does not take sin lightly and he also does not treat sin superficially. He does not simply say that these things are bad and that bad people need to stop being bad. From the very beginning of the book, God is concerned about the Israelites' idolatrous worship. He points out that all the disastrous displays of sin that we experience in our lives have much more to do with our identity and worship than our behavior and action. The problem does not lie in behavior in and of itself, but rather in the heart behind it. Sin is rampant not only out there in the world but also in the deepest parts of our hearts. Micah will keep bringing us back to God's diagnosis of what is really happening underneath all the injustice we see with our naked eyes. That will be more challenging for us, but more transformative of us.

- *Judgment.* Because of sin, God tells us through Micah that judgment is inevitable. He does not and will not overlook sin and its consequences. It is against his nature to put a blind eye to sin and its consequences, and pretend they do not exist. This is why Micah is not the easiest book to read—not because it is boring or seems irrelevant, but because it makes us feel uncomfortable. We cry out for justice to be served for the wrongs of others... but we are not so sure that justice should be done to us, for our wrongs. How even-handed are we when we demand justice? Micah makes us deal with these tough questions in life that we typically try to avoid. It is safe to say that if Micah does not make you feel uncomfortable, that is a clear sign that you are not reading it correctly. The inevitable consequences of judgment for oppression, evil, mistreatment of others, misuse of money, injustice, and abandonment are difficult to face. Micah is certainly not meant to be a feel-good read.

■ *Hope.* However, even in a book like this, we see that God invites us to see the hope of restoration. It may take a while but he promises it. And because we are confronted by our sin and God's judgment, we are well-placed to appreciate the message of hope. This restoration is a holistic* one—one that brings true, lasting, and full transformation. Sin forces us to see the ugliness of our hearts, but the promise of rescue deals with the restoration of all things, including our hearts! When we are able to experience this holistic transformation that comes to us as a gift, ultimately through the work of Jesus Christ, we then find that God-given power to carry out justice, love kindness, and walk humbly with him. As the Israelites looked forward to

> Christ is the One in whom all the tragedies, tensions, hopes, and laments of Micah find their resolution.

this coming restorative hope that was ultimately displayed in King Jesus, we have the opportunity to look back to this already-come rescue in King Jesus to move us into gospel obedience. So in each chapter of this book, we will not only be hearing from Micah; we will be pointed to Christ, since he is the One in whom all the tragedies, tensions, hopes, and laments of Micah find their fulfillment

---

* Words in gray are defined in the Glossary (page 159).

and their resolution. In seeing how Christ dealt with his people and hung on a cross for his people and rose again for his people, we will see the promises of Micah gloriously coming to pass.

The categories of sin, judgment, and hope will be helpful for you as you go through this book. Keep each in mind as you read each part of Micah, even if the focus is on one in particular. But these are not just categories that serve us as helpful guidelines for reading Micah. These are the categories for us to rightly evaluate what is going on in our lives as well. Sin is rampant, and judgment is inevitable, but hope is coming! Indeed, this hope has already come to us in Christ, who took on the inevitable judgment of our sin.

As we read this prophet in light of the coming of Jesus, we find that Micah can inspire and transform us to do the justice we yearn for, and love the kindness we long to see, as we walk through life with the God of consistent justice and overwhelming kindness.

1. THE END OF IDOLATRY

Peter Shaffer's play *Equus* is an exploration of worship. In centers on a psychiatrist by the name of Martin Dysart, who is caring for a client by the name of Alan. Alan's issue is that he does not quite understand what reality is. He is very energetic, joyful, and full of life as he pursues the object of his affection. The problem is that the object of his worship—his "god"—is a horse (hence the name of the play, *Equus*).

For Alan to become sane, Dysart needs to strip away the object of his affections, the very thing that makes him happy—but the horse is what has actually made Alan an individual who is full of life and filled with passion. As he grapples with whether to pursue Alan's sense of reality over his sense of happiness, Dysart himself goes through an existential struggle. He asks himself:

> "Who is really sane here? Is it this person who is engaged in worship, which is clearly a healthy thing, albeit for an animal? Or is it someone like me—someone who has no object of affection and who doesn't consider himself to believe in a god?"
>
> (*Equus*, pages 93-95)

In a postscript commentary, Shaffer goes on to talk about it in this way, as the author and evangelist Rebecca Manley Pippert recounts:

> "Unfashionable as it sounds, it is worship, he says, that sets us apart, that makes us unique. To be human is to worship. 'Real worship! Without worship you shrink. It's as brutal as that.'"
>
> (*Hope Has Its Reasons*, pages 64-65)

So where does one go to find trustworthy objects for devotion? Therein lies our problem: there are all sorts of objects of devotion that fight for our affections. And therein lay the problem for God's people, the Israelites, in Micah's day. As we shall see, they were engaged in idolatry—the worship of idols.

Word in History

The book of Micah begins with an explanation of what we are about to read: "The word of the LORD that came to Micah of Moresheth in the days of Jotham, Ahaz, and Hezekiah, kings of **Judah**" (**v 1***). In many of the other prophetic writings, the introductory phrase would be, for instance, "the word of Amos." Here it is "the word of the LORD." Micah's point here is to call the reader right from the beginning to give full attention to what is being said. This is "the word of the LORD." In the original Hebrew, it literally means "the word of the LORD that happened." In other words, it places an emphasis on a historical element. The word of God had happened in history and had come to Micah.

Micah is a professional prophet. There are some others who are not professional prophets, like Amos, who has another vocation. Micah's professional career, however, is to be a prophet. He is actually not from the region in which he speaks; he has come from outside to speak God's word (see Bruce Waltke's *Micah*, page 137).

The particular time the book speaks about can be discerned based on how it references three kings from Judah, the southern section of the promised land. (God's people had divided two centuries previously, during the reign of **Solomon**'s son Rehoboam—ever since, there had been two kingdoms: **Israel** to the north, centered on the capital of Samaria; Judah to the south, with Jerusalem as its capital.) Why is the time significant? Because it gives historical context. It is also significant that no kings of Israel are mentioned. In other words, they are

---

* All Micah verse references being looked at in each chapter part are in **bold**.

not even worthy to be mentioned in what is happening here because of the idolatrous activity they have led their nation into.

Nevertheless, Micah says that this is the word "which he saw concerning Samaria and Jerusalem." This word is coming to God's people for both Israel and Judah, for both Samaria and Jerusalem.

There are three key points in this section. First, Micah describes the judgment for idolatry. Secondly, he describes attachment to idolatry. Lastly, he describes rescue from idolatry. So if we are to grasp Micah's message to them and to us, we need first to think carefully about their idolatry, and ours.

Here is what makes the book challenging: Micah doesn't give readers any glimpse of restoration early on—it will only come later, and by way of rebuke. The deliverance will come through judgment. Restoration will come through rebuke. The resurrection will come through suffering. This is why a message like this is hard for any audience to receive.

Treading the High Places

First, the judgment for idolatry. This can be seen throughout the first chapter. Micah says that the LORD is coming out from his "holy temple" (presumably here meaning his heavenly dwelling-place, not the Jerusalem temple, though it could be either) as a witness against the inhabitants of the earth (primarily his people), and that he is going to provide cosmic judgment (**v 2**). What is the reason for or cause of this judgment? "The LORD is coming out of his place, and will come down and tread upon the high places of the earth" (**v 3**). "High places" were the **pagan** sanctuaries for idolatrous worship. And God warns that "All [his people's] carved images shall be beaten to pieces, all her wages shall be burned with fire, and all her idols I will lay waste, for from the fee of a prostitute she gathered them, and to the fee of a prostitute they shall return" (**v 7**).

The very existence of "high places" is the key to understanding what has gone wrong in Israel and Judah. God's people were told to worship God in Jerusalem, where the temple of God and his presence were—but they have instead chosen to worship somewhere else. Not only that, but they have also chosen to worship someone else. They worship someone else by going after carved images. If people choose to worship God in a way that is different from the one he sets out, very soon they will choose to worship a god who is different from the One who is real.

> People engage in injustice because of their idolatry.

Idolatry is choosing one's own will above God's will. It is giving ultimate allegiance—which deserves to be given to God alone—to another object of worship, another object of affection. That object could be wealth, influence, romance, power, control, approval, or comfort, and so on. Notice that **verse 7** promises that "her wages shall be burned with fire," because part of this idolatry—which is the reason why God's people are going to receive judgment from God—is idolatry centered around wealth. Not only that, but Micah also uses the metaphor of prostitution. This is the link between the people's idolatry and the people's injustice: they engage in injustice because of their idolatry of wealth and of sex. And God's judgment is going to come and destroy these idols.

Is God's Judgment Harsh?

Don't miss the scale of the judgment: it involves mountains melting and valleys splitting (**v 4**). This seems a little harsh. As long as people engage in good things, why should God come down so strongly and judge his own people? (By the way, Christians tend to think about judgment as related to the judgment of the world. It is important to know that God's judgment in the Bible is usually directed at those who are professing to be his people, because it is very possible to be born into a godly family, or to do all the "right rituals," and yet be so lost in idol-worship that in fact you have no relationship with God at all.

Here, the word of judgment is being spoken to and against the people of God in Samaria and Jerusalem.) Modern people have been brought up to find the notion of God's judgment very difficult. We like to hear about the mercy, forgiveness, grace, and love of God—but not his judgment, his wrath, or his anger. But the Bible clearly teaches that the God of mercy, forgiveness, **grace**, and love is at the same time the God who demonstrates anger and shows judgment against idolatry and idolaters.

So we must ask ourselves (because, even if we do not struggle with this, others who do will ask us), "How can I reconcile the anger of God with the love of God? How can I reconcile judgment with **justification**? How can I reconcile God's fury against his own people along with his grace? How is this possible?"

Becky Manley Pippert's insights are very helpful here. She points out that all loving persons are sometimes filled with anger—not just despite their love, but because of their love. The problem, Pippert notes, is that modern readers tend to be influenced by their own responses when analyzing God's, including his wrath. It is their own anger, their own irritability, their own wrath, their own fury, pettiness, and jealousies that they imagine, and this becomes a problem when analyzing God's anger and judgment. So if they are petty and emotionally lash out and explode on somebody with unrighteous anger, they think that that is how a wrathful God responds too.

The Bible, however, doesn't teach that God responds with unrighteous anger, but rather, with righteous anger. Pippert goes on to say:

> "Think of how we feel when we see someone we love ravaged by unwise actions or relationships. Do we respond with benign tolerance as we might toward strangers? Far from it. We are dead against whatever is destroying the one we love."
>
> (*Hope Has Its Reasons*, page 100)

She gives the example of a drug addict. Suppose you have a loved one—a sibling, parent, child, friend—who is addicted to drugs, and you can see how this addiction is ruining her life. She's going down this path of destruction and it will ruin her career and her future. Are you just going to come alongside of her with benign tolerance and say, "It's probably not a good idea for you to do this. Your life is really complex because of this. I'm just suggesting that it might not be a bad idea that you abandon all of that." And if they respond by saying, "Oh no, it's not a problem at all. It's recreational; I'm not addicted to this. My life is perfectly fine; there's no need to worry," thus revealing that they are in complete denial, would you respond with "tolerance" and say, "Oh, sorry, I didn't want to offend you. I just wanted to suggest that a different path may be something you could possibly consider, but you must do what seems best to you." No! As Pippert points out, love would cause you to respond:

> "'Do you know what you're doing to yourself? You become less and less yourself every time I see you.' I wasn't angry because I hated that person, I was angry because I cared. I was angry because I love them. I could have walked away, but love detests what destroys the beloved. Love destroys that which destroys the beloved. As a parent of grown-up children, I understand this more and more. When they're young kids, they don't have the competency to really, really mess up their lives. But once they're teenagers, they do have the ability to mess things up and to mess themselves up. They can worship idols that lead them down dark paths, even as the world cheers them on. Real love stands against the deception, the lie, the sin that destroys."
>
> (*Hope Has its Reasons*, page 100)

And love also stands against the person who hurts the child we love, who treats them unjustly. Why? Because anger is not the opposite of love. Anger flows out of love. Hatred or indifference is the opposite of love; anger is not. God may also be displaying this kind of love as he sees the wounds of Judah, his people (**v 9**). God will judge his people now, to remove their idols and return them to himself, so that they will not be left with their idols and be destroyed by them, and along with them, at his final judgment.

Looked at this way, when God judges his own people because of their idolatry and their injustice, it makes all the sense in the world, just as it makes all the sense in the world for us to not want to see our children engaged in activity that will destroy them, and to oppose those who are hurting them.

The Danger of Co-Existence

The pastor and theologian Tim Keller writes:

"The greatest danger, because it is such a subtle temptation which enables us to continue as church members and feel that nothing is wrong, is not that we become atheists, but that we ask God to co-exist with idols in our hearts."

(*Judges for You*, page 38)

This is the type of idolatry that God's people are engaged in. They have not actively, definitively rejected the God of the Scriptures. They have deliberately, consciously added other objects of worship to their worship of him. This is idolatry. It is, as God says through Micah, prostitution (**v 7**). It is spiritual adultery.

Among those who commit adultery, there are some who are no longer interested in their marriage. Once they've been exposed, they say, "This is the time for me to move on. I don't love you anymore. I don't want to be in this relationship." But many people who are engaged in adultery will say, "I still love you" to the spouse they have cheated on. They'll be sorry, and they'll protest their commitment—and then they'll cheat again.

Spiritually, that is the sort of idolatry that is adulterous. These people are saying, "God, we want to enjoy all the benefits of knowing you and being loved by you, and we do love you too—but we also want to be free to worship other things, too, because they make us happy." When we see their idolatry (and ours) in this way, we begin to see why God abhors it. We begin to grasp why God is angry over it. We begin to see why God speaks into this idolatry with judgment—because humans have such a strong attachment to their idols. There can be no rescue if there is not first removal of the objects of our idolatry. And, for the people in Micah's day, that would come through judgment.

Questions for reflection

1. "Idolatry is … giving ultimate allegiance—which deserves to be given to God alone—to another object of worship, another object of affection." None of us are immune from idol-worship. What are the three idols you are most prone to worship?

2. How would you explain the way God's anger and God's love work together to someone who is struggling with the idea that a loving God gets angry?

3. Why is asking the Lord to accept co-existence with other "gods" so easy to do?

PART TWO

An Idol Attachment

Micah has spoken about God's judgment against idolatry. Now he turns to consider their attachment to their idolatry.

An idol captures the hearts and imaginations of those who worship it. This is what it says in Psalm 1: "Blessed is the man who does not walk in the counsel of the wicked or stand in the way of sinners or sit in the seat of mockers. But his delight is in the law of the LORD, and on his law he meditates day and night" (v 1-2, NIV84). It is true that if a mind is shaped by meditation and reflection on God's word, then the life will be shaped as well, resulting in happiness. Yet people falsely assume that even if they are not shaped by meditation and reflection on God's word, there isn't anything else out there that is going to shape them. They think that they aren't being influenced and shaped—that they aren't delighting in or meditating on some other source. That is a complete lie.

Everyone is being influenced and shaped by other sources. Those who live in opposition to God are being influenced by standing in the way of sinners and sitting in the seat of mockers. Their hearts and imaginations are being captured and captivated by other objects of affection. Keller puts it this way in his unpublished resource, *Gospel Communication*:

"Fascism makes an idol of one's race and nationality. Socialism makes an idol of the state. Capitalism makes an idol of the free market. Humanism makes an idol of reason and science. Individualism makes an idol out of individual freedom. Traditionalism makes the family and tradition an idol."

(page 90)

What happens is that when all these corporate stories and idols are elevated, they begin to shape the lives of those who worship them. Consider then, what are those things for you?

Look at what it says in Micah's (or rather, God's) indictment. Micah **1:10-15** lists out names of towns that are hard to pronounce. Why are they included? First of all, because Micah is tracing out the path of the Assyrian army, which would ultimately end up overtaking Israel. These are all the places that its king, Sennacherib, would come to in order to take control over these regions. This is the path of the means of God's judgment.

Second, Micah is also trying to show that even though these cities have hopes based on their particular location, those hopes will not come to fruition. "Beth-le-aphrah," means the "house of dust" (**v 10**). Micah says to them, *Guess what? You're going to ultimately roll yourselves in dust.* He refers to "Shaphir" (**v 11**). The meaning of that word is "beauty town," and yet Micah tells them that they are going to live in nakedness and shame. "Zaanan" means "going forth town," but Micah says, "Do not come out." "Beth-ezel" means a "house of taking away," yet they "shall take away from you its standing place" (see Waltke, *Micah*, page 154). Micah uses deliberate puns to describe the ironic nature of the eventual destruction: the very thing that each place worships will be the source of its destruction and the place where its judgment is most clearly seen.

> Micah uses puns to describe the ironic nature of the eventual destruction.

These puns are mentioned throughout this list, and then **verse 15** says, "I will again bring a conqueror to you, inhabitants of Mareshah; the glory of Israel shall come to Adullam." The conqueror is referring to King Sennacherib, and the word "Mareshah" means "dispossess." Adullam was the cave where David went in order to flee the attack from Saul (1 Samuel 22:1). What Micah is saying is that his audience is going to want to flee because judgment is coming against their idolatry. There will be no place where there is reprieve or rest. This is the indictment and the judgment that is coming upon them: "Make yourselves bald and cut off your hair, for the children of your delight; make yourselves as bald as the eagle, for they shall go from you into exile" (Micah **1:16**). When he says, "Make yourselves bald and cut off your hair," it is a reference to shame.

Writing Our Storylines

The names of those towns in Micah's day may be distant from (and unpronounceable to) us, but they should provoke us to consider the way we too become attached to idols today. Personal idolatry really feeds on our desire to develop our identity and our security. Whatever the false promises are that are given by these counterfeit hopes, we gravitate toward them because we believe they will give us an answer for the deep longings within our hearts.

But there is also corporate, societal idolatry—the cultural narrative of a city or culture. The ultimate storyline of a city like Boston, my home, revolves around the idol of knowledge. Boston has an inferiority complex toward New York because New York has the best, the biggest, and the greatest of everything. What does Boston say? We don't care whether we have the best of everything; we just want to be the smartest person in the room. "Yeah, that's what you think in New York, but you know where you got that idea? You got it in Boston. The smartest people in New York are the ones who were educated and trained in Boston. That's just a fact." This is the way people think.

But this Bostonian assumption ends up affecting how we view people who engage in certain types of vocation that aren't considered "elite" or "superior" or full of contemplation. That work comes to have less value. The educated can begin to believe that they're doing work that's more important or that they themselves are more evolved. These corporate idols of knowledge, credentials, and career tend to support and undergird the injustices in our society. The things held in high esteem oftentime lead to injustice. Greed undergirds the disparities of wealth and poverty. Power undergirds racism and classism. Our corporate idols are behind all our injustices.

When people abandon the worship of the one true God to worship an idol, they begin to devise a storyline of their own. Yet they eventually start to suspect that perhaps they aren't as worthy as they thought. Their narrative tells them, "This is how you're supposed to be," but they fall short of the narrative, so they start feeling insecure. Then they start getting to the point where there is a sense of worthlessness. That leads to shame, which ultimately leads to anxiety. How then do people try to deal with that? One way is to try to escape from their circumstances. Another is to try to control their circumstances. But both ways still result in lives dominated by that idol, either in running from it or seeking to master it. Even if you see how you are worshiping an idol, it is harder than we naturally imagine not to stay attached to it.

The Advocate Arrives

Micah is 70% judgment and 30% restoration and deliverance. Here at the beginning, even careful readers of Micah 1 won't see a whole lot of allusions to restoration, salvation, or deliverance. This is why it's hard. In chapter 2 Micah warns readers, *I'm not going to be like that prophet that says things that will make people happy. I am a prophet of God's word; I have to speak God's word, as difficult as it is.* But the hope of rescue can be found.

This is a court case. God is the tribunal judge and he is calling the Israelites, who are the defendants. The Old Testament commentator Bruce Waltke talks about this section as a "call to a legal trial." He finds several elements in this call to trial:

1. A summons to the legal trial: "Hear, you peoples, all of you; pay attention, O earth, and all that is in it, and let the Lord GOD be a witness against you…" (**v 2**). Notice the legal language: Micah is saying, *Everyone, listen, here's the summons. Here's the subpoena. You're being summoned. I want you to come to the legal trial.*

2. A punitive epiphany: This means a kind of unfolding judgment that is still yet to come. Micah is giving a preview—an epiphany—of what that judgment will look like, in the case of a guilty verdict. The mountains will melt as God comes in judgment, and the valleys will "split open like wax before the fire" (**v 4**).

3. An accusation leveled against both Samaria and Jerusalem: "All this is for the transgression of Jacob and for the sins of the house of Israel. What is the transgression of Jacob? Is it not Samaria? And what is the high place of Judah? Is it not Jerusalem?" (**v 5**). This is the idolatry, the sin, the transgression.

4. The sentence: This is given in **verse 6**: "Therefore I will make Samaria a heap in the open country, a place for planting vineyards, and I will pour down her stones into the valley and uncover her foundations."

So the people are summoned, there's a picture of punishment, there is an accusation of the crime of idolatry, and then there is a sentence for that idolatry.

But where is the rescue? Well, as this legal trial proceeds, there is somebody who is trying to intercede as an advocate on behalf of the people. His name is Micah.

The meaning of the name "Micah" in the Hebrew is "Who is like Yahweh?" or "Who is like God?" And Micah comes to intercede. So as he thinks about the people and their sentence, he says, "For this I will lament and wail; I will go stripped and naked; I will make lamentation like the jackals, and mourning like the ostriches. For her wound is incurable, and it has come to Judah; it has reached to the gate of my people, to Jerusalem" (**v 8-9**).

God's judgment is very, very close to the fortification, to the gates, to the walls of this city where his people are protected. But Micah is trying to come on behalf of them as they've been called to a legal trial. Micah is trying to advocate for them, even to the point where he's willing to be stripped naked, to lament on their behalf. Micah understands that that is where the idolatry will lead—to the shame triad (for more on this see Ed Welch, *When People are Big and God is Small*, pages 170-171):

1. Feeling exposed

2. Rejection: feeling that you're not accepted

3. Contamination: feeling unclean

But Micah can't change anything. He can only lament; he can only join with them in being naked, rejected, and ashamed.

So where is the rescue?! Well, the story of Micah is, of course, part of the much larger story of the whole Bible, and as we read it in that context, we realize that there is somebody who has come into the courtroom—someone who, unlike Micah, can intercede, and somebody who actually can be an advocate. "Who is like Yahweh?" No one. No one is like Yahweh. Except then Jesus enters the courtroom, and he answers the question "Who is like Yahweh?" by saying, *No one is like Yahweh. And I am him. I am not like God. I **am** God.*

Not only that, but Jesus essentially came to earth to say, *I'm the Lord who will become naked so that you will be clothed with my righteousness. I am the Lord who will be rejected so that you will be fully accepted and embraced. I am the Lord who will become unclean and contaminated by your idolatry so that you might be rescued from its judgment and its attraction. I am the advocate.*

This advocate, this rescuer, is the only One who will be able to help us to dismantle our idols. He is the only One who can absorb the judgment of God so that we can be freed by the power of the gospel. The perfect legal advocate is the Lord himself. He is the only One who can be the answer to the question "Who is like God?" He is the only One who can free us from putting idols on the throne of our hearts, either in his place or co-occupying it with him. He is the only One who will fully satisfy everything that we're longing for.

Many people have a sense of worthlessness, shame, fear, anxiety, and depression. The world, the flesh, and the evil one tell them

over and over again, *You're no good.
You're ugly. You're worthless. You're
despicable. You're a nobody. You're
an utter failure. You'll never please
your parents. You'll never gain their
approval. You'll never get anywhere.
You're nobody.* That's the voice that
they hear over and over. And outside
of a saving relationship to God, in

> Micah could do
> no more than
> lament. Jesus
> came to remove
> our lament.

one sense much of that is true. But in response, Jesus comes into the
room and says these powerful words of truth: *I won't just enter into
sharing with you your shame and nakedness; I'll take them from you.*
God the Father says, *You are my beloved. Nothing can change that.
You are my beloved. You are my chosen possession. In you I am well
pleased, because I was well pleased with my beloved Son, who absorbed the judgment that you deserved so that you might receive the
acceptance and embrace that he deserved.*

This is the picture of the gospel. This is the power that will root out
and dismantle all the appetites for the other objects of affection, both
now and forever. Micah could do no more than join the lament. Jesus
came in order to remove our lament.

Questions for reflection

1. What is the cultural storyline that dominates your own city or society?

2. Have you experienced an area in which you have been idolatrous,
and then found that that area is the place where life falls apart?

3. How does comparing Micah and Jesus move you to appreciate
Jesus more deeply and worship him more joyfully?

2. OPPRESSION CALLED OUT

Much like the opening chapter, the second chapter of Micah feels strange and uncomfortable to modern readers. We will need to get used to this as we take the time to explore this book. These are verses that we may be shocked to find in the Bible at all, especially when we consider that they are addressed to the people of God:

- "Thus says the LORD: behold, against this family I am devising disaster, from which you cannot remove your necks..." (**2:3**)

- "In that day they shall take up a taunt song against you..." (**v 4**)

- "Arise and go, for this is no place to rest..." (**v 10**)

Micah's central message revolves around God making everything right, but in the process, he will, because he has to, confront his hearers—in his day, but also in ours—with wrongs. Micah is revealing to us that there is a process: in short, restoration is on its way, but it's going to come through rebuke. It must. We may want to jump quickly to restoration because that is what sets our hearts at ease. But God is revealing to us, through Micah, that true restoration waits. It takes time. It's going to come through rebuke.

Chapter 2 is only a snapshot of some of the ways that Micah essentially gets in our faces all throughout the book. I want to be upfront with you and give you a health warning at the beginning of this commentary: there will (or should) be several moments in this book where you're going to feel deeply challenged. You're not going to want to hear it. It's going to shake us up, but don't shut down out of fear, frustration, or fatigue. Keep in mind God's way of executing restoration: restoration comes through rebuke. This is how reality works. In life, when there is a problem, things may well get worse before they get better. The life-saving cure follows a diagnosis of something life-threatening. In the book of Micah, the cure wonderfully comes. Restoration will follow rebuke.

In this chapter, we will explore the topic of oppression. The following three movements will guide our thinking regarding oppression as Micah walks us through God's indictment:

1. Oppression is real.

2. How oppression might make us feel.

3. What God is going to do to deal with oppression in the end.

Oppression Is Real

First, oppression is real. **Verses 1-2** speak of "those who devise wickedness and work evil on their beds! … They covet fields and seize them, and houses, and take them away; they oppress a man and his house, a man and his inheritance." When we think about oppression, our minds typically drift towards some caricature of evil—somebody with malice in their eyes who intentionally preys on the weak. Sometimes oppression does take that form. And the disgust that we experience as a result of that intentional and explicit oppression is easily shared by many. We find it easy to say of those things, "Woe to those who devise [them]" (**v 1**). Some do calculate wickedness—they "work evil on their beds." Some do evil even in their sleep because they are thinking about it so much.

But there is more. This passage actually goes to much more depth to describe all kinds of oppression that may be implicit rather than explicit, and subtle rather than obvious: "They covet fields and seize them," says Micah (**v 2**). The context is important to consider here. This was an agrarian society. So a person's fields would have served a very specific and important function. They were the means of opportunity and how you made a living and a life for yourself and your family. So if someone's field was seized, even if not out of malice and explicit ill intent, they would be severely crippled and put at a disadvantage. They would have taken a huge hit.

In today's culture, it is not every day that people steal others' fields but there are similar dynamics at play that create the same disparities of opportunity. Whether you live in the ancient or modern world, such evil acts get displayed in all human societies and communities. There's another example in **verse 9**: "The women of my people you drive out from their delightful houses; from their young children you take away my splendor forever." That happens in our societies. We are not so distant from Micah's day as we might like to think. Like back then, today women and the children of the poor suffer great disadvantages. Women are more likely to live in poverty than men are. The causes of these realities are never simple, but nonetheless, there are certain structural realities in life, both ancient and modern life, that allow both obvious and subtle forms of oppression to exist.

The Powerlessness of Poverty

When you are poor, you do not have much power. The Bible tells us this as well, which is the reason why God is so exercised to stand up for the poor and to insist that his people do likewise. For the poor, the little that they do have just keeps getting taken away. That seems to be God's charge in **verse 8**, which pictures how his people see everything others have as potential plunder: "My people have risen up as an enemy; you strip the rich robe from those who pass by trustingly with no thought of war."

When you begin to see the kinds of dynamics that were in play in the society that Micah spoke into, **verse 10** starts to make a lot more sense: "Arise and go, for this is no place to rest, because of uncleanness that destroys with a grievous destruction." When you constantly lack opportunities, it just destroys you. No matter where you turn, you cannot rest. There is no place to rest.

Again, we have to confront the truth that those kinds of dynamics, that kind of **endemic** and systemic oppression, have not passed away with the ancient world. A recent essay by Linda Tirado, who wrestled for decades with poverty, went viral. In it, she describes her life as a wife and mom battling poverty:

"A rest is a luxury for the rich. I get up at 6, go to school, then work. Then I get the kids and pick up my husband. Then I have half an hour to change and go to job two. I get home from that around 12:30 a.m. Then I have the rest of my classes and work to tend to. I'm in bed by 3. I never get a day off from work unless I'm fairly sick, but that's not the worst part. Nobody gives enough thought to depression. You have to understand that we know that we will never not feel tired. We'll never feel hopeful. We will never get a vacation, ever. We don't apply for certain jobs because we know we can't afford to look nice enough to hold them. I would make a super legal secretary, but I've been turned down more than once because I don't fit the image of a firm. I'm not beautiful. I have missing teeth and skin that looks like it will when you live on B12 [vitamin supplements], coffee, and no sleep. Beauty is a thing you get when you can afford it, and that's how you get the job you need in order to be beautiful."

(Linda Tirado, "This is Why Poor People's Bad Decisions Make Perfect Sense," 2013, accessed 9/1/17: http://bit.ly/1gNmXOu)

Maybe you can identify with this all to easily. But all too many of us would have difficulty relating to Tirado's experiences; we may feel sympathy, but there will be very little common ground for empathy. Of course, many of the advantages and luxuries that we have (that Tirado mentions) are achieved legally, fair and square. However, the acquisitions that Micah is describing in chapter 2 were also obtained legally; but not in a way that was (as Micah would say) oppression-free.

In ancient times, it was perfectly legal to take someone's field if they defaulted on a loan—or their robe, or house, or whatever. So **verse 1** says that, "When the morning dawns, they perform it." These "repossessions" happened when the morning dawned—in broad daylight. No one was sneaking around in the shadows because all this was perfectly within the lines of law—and yet Micah still chose to call it oppression. This goes to show that Micah's declaration and unpacking of oppression is much more comprehensive (and therefore confrontational for us) than we may think. There are nuanced realities of oppression, and Micah wants to reveal them through these verses.

There are two things that the text is *not* saying. It is not saying that there is anything inherently wrong with economic gain. And it is not insinuating that you ought to feel guilty because of your gain and advantages. What it *is* challenging us to do is to acknowledge the fact that our possessions often come at the expense of someone who lacks the advantages that we do have—even the fair ones that can be celebrated. We can easily oppress someone else without an ounce of malice in our hearts. It can be very subtle and yet it can be very real.

> We can easily oppress someone without an ounce of malice in our hearts.

Oppression is real not only because someone is devising it explicitly or obviously. Oppression is not real only for the person who thinks about it in his or her sleep. Oppression is real even when it is not deliberate or malicious.

Exploring this probably makes a lot of people feel very uncomfortable, especially when gaining advantages at all costs seems to be the name of the game for today's world. Let us now actually take this opportunity to explore how this real oppression often makes people feel.

You Don't Want to Hear This (But You Need To)

In **verse 6**, Micah gives his listeners a voice: "'Do not preach'—thus they preach—'one should not preach of such things; disgrace will not overtake us.'" Maybe you're thinking, *Don't preach about this. You*

*don't need to preach about this. God is not that concerned about this
stuff. I'm not doing anything wrong. I know these things are a blessing. And doesn't he just really want me to be happy?* Micah deals with
that thought in **verse 7**: "Should this be said, O house of Jacob? Has
the LORD grown impatient? Are these his deeds? Do not my words do
good to him who walks uprightly?" If we think that God does not
care about these issues that we have explored so far, then we do not
really know much about him, his words, or his deeds. If we are saying
that all he cares about is our happiness, then apparently we are not
walking uprightly. That is what this verse helps us to notice and feel.

For Americans, this really is difficult to understand. That is what
happens when a concept like the "American dream" gets equated
with God's dream for mankind. The pursuit of happiness is not his
will for our lives and those things that contribute to our happiness
(for which, so often, we can simply read "wealth") are not necessarily
his deeds. One of the biggest mistakes we have made in attempting
to understand God and his will for us is to equate the market with
the will of God. The market is wonderful in so many ways, of course,
but we have to remember that Adam Smith's "invisible hand" is not
God's hand.

Oppression is real whether or not we talk about it, whether or not
it exhausts us, whether or not we've found ways to ignore it. It is real.
We can either choose to be real with it or just close our eyes and ignore the reality that constantly surrounds us. Inequality, in every sense
of that word, is worse today than it has ever been.

Again, none of this is easy to hear and none of this has easy answers. Micah was not written to soothe those who want a comfortable, low-stress life. And that is who Micah was speaking to: "If a man
should go about and utter wind and lies, saying, 'I will preach to you
of wine and strong drink,' he would be the preacher for this people!"
(**v 11**). It is easy to give and receive "wine and strong drink." But what
we need is not easy; we need truth. As complicated and uncomfortable as oppression and the idea that we may be the oppressors might

be, we are still called to wrestle with the questions: What do we do about our neighbors who experience silent oppression each and every single day? How do we care for them? How do we reach out to the poor and the powerless? Do our hearts truly break because of the reality of oppression, or would we rather turn a blind eye for our own peace of mind?

Questions for reflection

1. How has this section made you re-evaluate your view of what oppression is, and how you might be part of it?

2. Do you instinctively tend to blame poverty on the individual, or on the system? To what extent is your tendency a helpful reaction, and how might it be unhelpful or unfair?

3. What might the attitude of verses 7 and 11 look like in your own thoughts or life?

PART TWO

I Have a Problem with the Bible

Try to imagine for a moment, as uncomfortable and unnerving as it may be, how refreshing these verses would be to you if you were truly poor and powerless. (Maybe you do not need to imagine this—it may be your reality.) Imagine hearing Micah utter these words when you are someone who feels constantly stuck in life, without any help—without even the awareness to seek help because you lack the contacts, the knowledge, the power to do so.

This is the reality of the poor that not many of us are exposed to on a daily basis. To be poor is not automatically to be lazy or dependent, despite the stereotypes; but to be poor is, in most places and at most times, to be stuck without the ability to chase a dream or entertain realistic hope. If that were your life, then Micah **2:3-4** would be a breath of fresh air to you, because it would be a shimmering hope in the distance. It would be a picture of power that you did not know you could ever have dreamed of. It would be a pointer to a God who does not oppress you, and will not stand to see you oppressed.

It is hard to read the Bible from that perspective if you have not experienced that life. But it is critical to seek to do so. Brian Zahnd, a pastor in Missouri, really helped me see it from this perspective. I shall quote him at some length:

"I have a problem with the Bible. I am an ancient Egyptian. A comfortable Babylonian. A Roman in his villa. I'm not a Hebrew slave suffering in Egypt ... a conquered Judean deported to Babylon. I'm not a first century Jew living under Roman occupation.

"One of the most remarkable things about the Bible is that [it tells] a narrative ... from the perspective of the poor [and] oppressed ... This is [its] subversive genius ... [But] what happens if those on top read themselves into the story, not as imperial Egyptians, Babylonians, and Romans, but as the Israelites? That's when you get the bizarre phenomenon of the elite and entitled using the Bible to endorse their dominance as God's will. This is Roman Christianity after **Constantine**. This is **Christendom** on crusade … This is the whole history of European colonialism. This is **Jim Crow**. This is the American prosperity gospel … This is making the Bible dance a jig for our own amusement …

"Imagine this: A powerful charismatic figure arrives on the world scene … announcing a new arrangement … where those at the bottom are to be promoted and those on top are to have their lifestyle 'restructured.' I can imagine the Bangladeshis saying, 'When do we start?!' and the Americans saying, 'Hold on now, let's not get carried away!' …

"And that's the challenge I face in reading the Bible. I'm not the Galilean peasant. Who am I kidding! I'm the Roman in his villa and I need to be honest about it. I too can hear the gospel of the kingdom as good news (because it is!), but first I need to admit its radical nature and not try to tame it to endorse my inherited entitlement.

"I am … relatively wealthy … Which is fine, but it means I have to work hard at reading the Bible right … I don't fancy myself as **Elijah** calling down fire from heaven. I'm more like Nebuchadnezzar, [and I need to humble myself] lest I go insane …

"What does the Bible ask of me? Voluntary poverty? Not necessarily. But certainly the Bible calls me to deep humility—a humility demonstrated in hospitality and generosity.

"I have a problem with the Bible, but all is not lost. I just need to read it standing on my head … If I can accept that the Bible is trying to lift up those who are unlike me, then perhaps I can read the Bible right."

(Brian Zahnd, "My Problem With the Bible," 2014, accessed 9/1/17: https://brianzahnd.com/2014/02/problem-bible/)

Maybe we, too, can read the Bible that way, and can begin to feel differently about oppression. If we did so, we would read God's words promising an end to oppression and feel the joy of it, even as we experience the discomfort of our complicity in it.

An End to Oppression

And God *is* going to bring an end to oppression:

> "Therefore thus says the LORD: behold, against this family I am devising disaster, from which you cannot remove your necks, and you shall not walk haughtily, for it will be a time of disaster. In that day they shall take up a taunt song against you and moan bitterly, and say, 'We are utterly ruined; he changes the portion of my people; how he removes it from me! To an apostate he allots our fields.'" (**v 3-4**)

It turns out that oppression is on a short leash, along with the arrogance and pride of the powerful and the rich. This is either going to be really, really good news to you or really, really bad news. There is no middle ground here. If you are poor, this is the dawn of a new day breaking on the horizon. If you are rich, it is ruin. Disaster is heading our way and we cannot do anything to save our necks.

Everything the wealthy have will be lost, Micah promises in **verse 5**: "Therefore you will have none to cast the line by lot in the assembly of the LORD." Remember that Micah is doing his ministry right before the Israelites are sent off to Babylon in exile. Basically, what God is telling the rich here is, *Look, there is going to come a day when I will bring you back from Babylon to your own land, back to Israel. When I do that, you will have no share in that land. Everything you worked for—the little empires you built for yourselves, all the wealth you stored away—is all going to be taken. I am going to recast the line by lot to divide up the land; and you will get nothing.*

Then to top it off, he essentially says in **verse 4**, *As I do that to you, I am going to take the poor. I am going to make them rise from the rubble to delight over your plight. They will taunt you over your destruction with your own lament.* The rich will be crying out, "We are utterly ruined" and the poor will be taunting them. The crushed will rise to mock the no-longer-powerful ones.

Breaking Through the Breach

This is awful! This is terrible! But it is only as we respond in that way that we can begin to hear the wonderful, ground-breaking, earth-shattering news: beyond getting worse, things will get better. Beyond rebuke comes restoration.

So the LORD promises through his prophet in **verses 12-13**:

"I will surely assemble all of you, O Jacob; I will gather the **remnant** of Israel; I will set them together like sheep in a fold, like a flock in its pasture, a noisy multitude of men. He who opens the breach goes up before them; they break through and pass the gate, going out by it. Their king passes on before them, the LORD at their head."

The doom and gloom of Micah 2 was paving the way for a shining, shimmering hope. We need this, badly. But we also desperately need the verses leading up to this so that we can humbly appreciate the hope we see here. We are not supposed to have warm, fuzzy feelings when the Bible calls us sheep. It is the farthest thing from being a compliment. Sheep are animals who need help, who cannot last long left to themselves.

> When the Bible calls us sheep, it is the farthest thing from being a compliment.

And here is the ultimate hope: a Shepherd is on his way who gathers his people together. He will burst through the breach, the gap, and burst open the gates of oppression to lead us to the dawn of a new day. And as our hearts leap with joyous anticipation for this Shepherd, we can look forward a few hundred years. A charismatic figure, Jesus, shows up in Israel, and walks around calling himself the Good Shepherd. And he says, *I'm bringing in a new order; the last are first now; the poor are blessed; the oppressed are free.* How does he bring in this new order? *I will take the last spot, the lowest place, myself,* he says. *Do you want riches? Make me poor. Do you want strength? Strip me of all of mine and make me weak.*

And yet when the elites, the wealthy and the influential heard him say all this, instead of being grateful, they hated him because what he did exposed how selfish, callous, hardened, and arrogant their own hearts had become. They were made to feel very, very uncomfortable, so they asked him to keep quiet. But he would not. So they said, *We have to do something about radical Jesus of Nazareth. Let us take his robe off his back. Let us beat him. Let us make fun of him. Let us mock him with his own lament. Shove a crown of thorns on his head, nail him to a cross, and send him to his ruin.* And he responded, *And I will let you do all of it. I will let you do it because it is the only way to save you. I cannot deal with oppression without destroying the oppressors unless I take the consequences on myself, and I will do it. I will do it for the oppressed, that they may be freed, but also for the oppressors, that they may also be freed. That is how much I love my sheep.* That is what God has done to deal with oppression.

> God is looking for people to use what they have, at expense to themselves, for the benefit of others.

And he is not done yet, either. He is still looking for "a noisy multitude" to join him. He is still looking for people—those who know what it is like to gain at the expense of somebody else when they did not deserve it—to use what they have, at expense to themselves, for the benefit of others. That is what he wants. That is his vision. That is his desire. He will burst through the gates of oppression and open the breach. He will lead you through.

What does this mean for us? How will all of this impact and shape us? How will this work of God in Christ move us to see all the ways that we contribute to oppression all around us? It will force us to ask some tough questions, and we will need boldness to answer them honestly. It means that decisions in life won't be easy. It at least means that we need to soberly assess the way we live our lives as those who understand the heart of the gospel—who understand that the gift of life that we have came at the expense of someone else's comfort and life—so that we move to the direction of a self-giving life that seeks the good of others. This is the good news that we have in the midst of oppression. We have a way through it and out of it and beyond it. Jesus has shown us the way. He first demonstrated it himself by giving up his riches, comfort, and advantages, so that we may flourish. It is only when we realize this reality that has come to us in the name of salvation that we can then move out to extend this to others with joy and gratitude. As God's people, we should be quicker to see oppression, and quicker to admit to ways we may have unconsciously contributed to it. As God's people, we are freed to give what we would otherwise seek to grasp, and to give up what we once strived to get.

Think about something you can use at your expense for someone else's good, and then use it that way. With that, God will gather what we give, together with what others give, and he will start the process of opening up that breach, bursting through the gates of oppression and leading us to a brand new day.

Questions for reflection

1. "I need to admit to [the Bible's] radical nature and not try to tame it to endorse my inherited entitlement" (Brian Zahnd). in what ways will the Bible become both more exciting and more challenging to us if we refuse to "tame it"?

2. Do you recognize the description of yourself as a sheep? In what way?

3. "As God's people, we are freed to give what we would otherwise seek to grasp, and to give up what we once strived to get." What will this look like in your life today? How will your bank statement reflect these truths?

3. POWER RECONSIDERED

Micah's name means, "Who is like God?" Over and over again, readers of Micah see that the answer to that question is that no one is. Both the gods of pagan worship and Micah's own leaders are clearly not like God. Even Micah, although he has characteristics more aligned with God's character, is obviously ultimately not like God. These same ideas continue to unfold throughout the rest of the book. And when we reach the New Testament, we discover that even Jesus is not "like God"; he *is* God. Made incarnate, Jesus became like us; but we are not like him, for we are not like God, and he is God.

Micah is, as we have seen, speaking difficult words to a nation that has gone off the rails. They have neglected their identity and responsibility as God's people. Micah 1 showed how injustice in Israel was rooted in the idolatry of Israel. Chapter 2 showed how Israel was a place of oppression. Because of the idolatry, the injustice, and the oppression, God was bringing judgment. And chapter 3 now shows how idolatrous oppression is carried out through the misuse of power.

Micah and Social Justice

Like Micah, people today are exercised by issues of social injustice. Even though they might not like the general doctrine of justice or judgment, whenever somebody says, "Hey, here's a social injustice," most modern people will speak against it. Whenever they do that, they are in fact lining up with the God of the Bible, because God

speaks against social injustice. He doesn't like it when people misuse their power in order to manipulate the disadvantaged. Humans
are supposed to utilize their power to help the hurting, just as their
Creator did and does. But among the national leaders and even the
religious leaders of Micah's time, men were leveraging their God-given
power for selfish ends. This is what God, through Micah, is speaking
out against.

The concept of power might seem a little foreign to you. It might
seem a little intangible and philosophical. Yet every human being has
some level of power—even infants and children. (Ever seen parents
who dote over their young infants? There is a certain level of power
there. Those infants can attract their parents' attention and have
some leverage and influence over them, even though those children
don't realize it.)

Consider the power dynamics of a family. Every member of the
family exercises some level of power. Whether it's by the firstborn or
the youngest child in sibling rivalry or in the relationship between a
parent and child—everyone has a level of influence and power within
the family. Healthy families can utilize that power dynamic in ways
that build up the family. Unhealthy families don't know how to use influence and power well, which leads to the breakdown or even break-
up of family life.

There are also, of course, power dynamics in the workplace. There
are official power structures, like the hierarchy of supervisors and em-
ployers and employees. There are also unofficial power structures; people share the same rank but differ in the kind of influence and leverage
that they have. Perhaps one person has a more dynamic personality and
is a little more favored by the supervisor, and therefore, compared to his
peers, has a greater level of power in the workplace.

The church is not immune to power dynamics either. There are
members of the church who have official responsibilities like the pas-
tors, elders, deacons, and staff members. There are also unofficial
powers, enjoyed or even wrestled over by those who speak up more

or share a little more; or by those who have been members longest (or are willing to argue the longest).

The point is that everyone has power, to a greater or lesser degree. It is a gift from God, and his people are called to employ it for his glory and for the common good.

When most people think about power, they think of Lord Acton's famous dictum, "Power corrupts; absolute power corrupts absolutely." In discussions of power, people always bring that up and say, "If absolute power corrupts absolutely, we ought to get rid of power." But you can't get rid of power. It exists in any human relationship and organization. And we shouldn't want to get rid of it, even if we could. It's a gift that can be used for human flourishing. It's the same with authority. Some people don't like authority and want to get rid of it. But authority is not what is terrible; it's the abuse of that authority that is the problem. Power is not what is intrinsically sinful; it's the abuse of power that needs to be addressed.

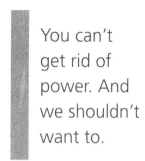

You can't get rid of power. And we shouldn't want to.

Micah's words reveal what God thinks about power gone wrong, and the ways that his people can reharness and understand power for its intended purpose. His message here breaks down into three main points: the misuse of power, the proper use of power, and the renewal of power.

The Misuse of Power

Micah begins in **3:1**, "Hear, you heads of Jacob and rulers of the house of Israel! Is it not for you to know justice?" This is similar to chapter 1, in which Micah called the cities and the representatives of Samaria and Jerusalem to trial. Again, Micah gets their attention: the "heads" and "rulers" of the nation are being summoned to trial, and so there will be an accusation and a sentence.

God has appointed these leaders to rule his people and to bring about flourishing. The national leaders are the ones who are supposed to know about justice. They are the ones who should exercise their power and God-given authority for the common good. Obviously, they haven't done so, and that is why the indictment comes: "Is it not for you to know justice?" (**3:1**) .

Micah is saying, *You are the ones who have been assigned to act justly and to be compassionate and merciful, especially for the people who have been marginalized.* But these leaders have lost sight of the very task that they were called to carry out. Listen to the stunning description of their misused power in **verses 2-3**: "You who hate the good and love the evil, who tear the skin from off my people and their flesh from off their bones, who eat the flesh of my people, and flay their skin from off them, and break their bones in pieces and chop them up like meat in a pot, like flesh in a cauldron." The Assyrians, the power in Micah's time, under the rule of Sennacherib, had a common practice: they captured their enemies and flayed their skin, while they were still alive. So God is being symbolic here. He's basically saying, *I know that you're my national magistrates, but you are metaphorically doing to your own people what the enemy is doing to your people.* That is the worst indictment there can be: that the leaders of a people are acting as the enemies of the people. The leaders have the privilege of potentially harnessing this gift of great power, but instead they have misused it.

Here's a working definition of misused power: it is *taking the in-fluence God has given you for the sake of the common good, and using it against others for selfish gain.* And in Micah's day, the misuse of power was tragically widespread, as he says in **verse 11**: "[The nation's] heads give judgment for a bribe; its priests teach for a price; its prophets practice divination for money; yet they lean on the LORD and say, 'Is not the LORD in the midst of us? No disaster shall come upon us.'" Now the accusation is also against the religious leaders and not just the political leaders. It may seem as if they are simply performing their job. From another perspective, however, they are abusing their power: "Thus says the LORD concerning the prophets who lead my people astray, who cry 'Peace' when they have something to eat, but declare war against him who puts nothing into their mouths" (**v 5**). Micah is saying that when these religious leaders receive some monetary benefit for the work they've been called to do, they then speak a warm, comforting message of peace to the people. But when they don't receive a fee for the work they do, then they preach war. Their prophecies can be bought. They misuse their power to line their pockets.

I have been in pastoral ministry for 25 years, and I know that there's always a temptation, when seeing a crowd, to soften the message so that it will be something that they want to hear. Even if God is effectively telling you, *This is the message you are called preach*, it's easier to soften it than deliver it unedited—especially if the audience includes potential donors. So Micah is due some credit, for he preaches faithfully regardless of whether his audience has less privilege or whether they can offer resources to support ministry. He certainly could not be accused of preaching what people want to hear! And his message here for the religious leaders is that they, like him, should be preaching the same message to both groups: to those who can give much and those who can only give little. The danger and temptation is always there: to preach war and judgment to those who have no food to offer, and a message of peace and comfort to those who can provide necessities. This is a lot subtler than most people think. It's not so black and white; it's not so easily identifiable. Yet it matters.

If You Don't Listen, I Won't Listen

What is God's response to misused power? "Then they will cry to the LORD, but he will not answer them; he will hide his face from them at that time, because they have made their deeds evil" (**v 4**). In other words, God says that he will not hear these religious leaders when they call out to him. God will not listen to them, because when the marginalized are in need of support from these leaders, they do not listen to them. **Verses 6-7** further describe the nature of this silence from God. God is saying, *You don't listen to the people who are weak and lack privilege. If, therefore, you are engaging in social injustice, why should I listen to your plea? And if you will not speak truth to those who need truth from you, why would you expect truth from me when you look for it? You chose to be silent when you should have spoken; you will find silence from me when you wish I would speak.*

Robert Fuller was once a college president, and he now runs a large not-for-profit organization, and has written two very insightful books, *Somebodies and Nobodies* and *All Rise*. This is what he says:

"Characteristics such as religion, race, gender, and age are merely excuses for discrimination, never its ultimate cause."

(*All Rise*, pages 5-6)

This is important to know, because these are features that most people think are ultimately the root causes of all discrimination. He goes on to say that there is something underneath all these "excuses for discrimination"—but what he doesn't realize is that he's trying to look for the sin underneath the sin, the idolatry underneath the act. Racism is actually a fruit of something deeper. Classism is a consequence of something deeper. There is a sin underneath each sin. According to Fuller:

All "isms" occur when people overuse and misuse power.

"There is one common root that combines all of these isms together, and that is the presumption and assertion of rank to the detriment of others."

(*All Rise*, pages 5-6)

Society needs to understand and unearth the ongoing use—misuse— of power and advantage that transcends race, gender, religion, and class. That's what is at the root of all these issues—what Fuller calls "rankism." All these "isms" occur when people overuse and misuse the power and domination of their rank in order to subordinate and dismiss another group of people or individual.

The problem, again, is not with power or authority; it is the abuse of power, as Fuller argues:

"When people abuse their power to demean or disadvantage those they outrank, that will lead to indignity."

(*All Rise*, page 10)

It doesn't matter what the issue is. And Fuller would have concurred with the Old Testament prophets' analysis of the religious leaders in their time. Isaiah, a contemporary of Micah, also speaks to the rulers in Jerusalem in Isaiah 1:17: "Learn to do good; seek justice, correct oppression; bring justice to the fatherless, plead the widow's cause." They have been given a responsibility to be just and to help the people who lack rank, power, and privilege. But, as Micah lays bare, they have not discharged that responsibility.

A Question of Privilege

Some readers might say to themselves, "Okay, I get it. Micah is describing the religious leaders of his day. Maybe he's describing some of the political leaders of our day, too. But what potential danger of falling into the same category is there for me—just a normal guy in a normal life?"

But, as the commentator David Prior describes it, the central charge in Micah 2 against these people is that "they had a corrupt and callous lifestyle" (*Joel, Micah, Habakkuk*, page 139). Micah is talking about people who demonstrate a consistent lifestyle born of an attitude that views power as something at our own disposal, to serve the self with.

And all of us are or can easily become such people. In his famous work *The Will to Power*, the 19th-century nihilistic philosopher Friedrich Nietzsche wrote:

"My idea is that every specific body strives to become master over all space and to extend its force; to thrust back all that resists its extension." (*The Will to Power*, Line 639)

There is one area where this happens very subtly—privilege. It is worth evaluating our own hearts. Andy Crouch has written a book entitled *Playing God*. It's a very helpful book for anyone interested in understanding these issues of power. In it, he writes, "Privilege is a special kind of power." All people have privilege, but not everyone realizes that privilege is a special kind of power. Some readers might say to themselves, "I'm not in a place of high rank with influence and power"—but almost all of us are privileged, to some degree. Crouch goes on to say:

"The best way I know to define privilege is the ongoing benefits of past successful exercises of power." (*Playing God*, page 150)

Those "past exercises of power" include power exercised by parents, ancestors, or certain institutions.

Crouch gives the illustration of an author's royalties. Publishers and authors determine what the royalty should be depending on an author's status. So authors hope that their books sell well, because, if so, then they get 15, 18, maybe even 22 or 26% of each sale as a royalty. If a book sells well, its author receives benefits from it, even without any additional effort. That's their privilege. The act of power was exercised earlier in the agreement of the contract—the privilege is enjoyed later, as the book sells. Likewise, everyone is placed in a particular position through privileges we enjoy, or privileges we lack, because of previous uses (or abuses) of power.

All this raises hard questions. In what ways could we possibly be misusing our power and privilege for personal gain, while minimizing and demeaning others who have less rank and fewer resources? That is where the personal application needs to come. Even though we may not go around flaying people, most of us have a lot more rank, power, and privilege than we know. Is there a possibility that we are misusing the resources and gifts that God has given to us?

Questions for reflection

1. Is there anyone you know who is exercised about social justice, and hasn't realized that God is too? How might this help you to engage them in a positive conversation about Christianity?

2. Power "is a gift that can be used for human flourishing"—but it can also be misused. What mistaken views of power have you seen, in your own life or in the lives of those around you?

3. What privileges do you enjoy, and what power does that bring you? What will it look like for you to use that power for the good of others, rather than for your own gain?

PART TWO

A Positive Use of Power

Micah does not just call out the abuse of power he sees around him. He is also, himself, an embodiment of the proper use of power. Here is how he describes himself in Micah **3:8**: "As for me, I am filled with power, with the Spirit of the LORD, and with justice and might, to declare to Jacob his transgression and to Israel his sin." Micah is the inverse of the false prophets. He is somebody who is filled with power and the Spirit of God, and he is filled with justice and might. He is not filled with injustice, the abuse of power, or his own identity. Rather, he is filled with power that comes from the Spirit of the LORD. This is similar to the language of Isaiah 42 and 44, where Isaiah talks about the messianic figure and says that the Spirit of the Lord will be upon him. To do what? To engage in acts of justice.

Micah wanted to leverage his Spirit-given power for the common good. As we consider the proper use of our own power, we should ask ourselves, "Do I use whatever rank or power I have to engage in a proper use of power, or in a self-serving, self-aggrandizing, self-protecting power play?" Unless we are very self-aware, most of us don't even realize when we are doing the latter—and that includes church leaders. But we do do it. For instance, as we have conversations at work, most of us calibrate our co-workers' value and worth relative to the specific context; if we sense that they have little more rank and influence and favor than us in that context, then we often engage in a power play to come out top. Equally if we sense that they have greater power, then we will treat them differently than someone who has no power, as we want to enjoy the patronage of that power. Add to that the dynamics of class, rank, gender, age, and race, and a complex dynamic arises in which it is easy for a power play to take place without us even really noticing we are doing it. So it's necessary to be very self-aware.

Most of us will have encountered someone who was condescending because of our younger age or lack of experience or perhaps because of our particular race, culture, or gender. Many of us have been perpetrators as well victims of such misuses of power. In what subtle ways might you be like that?

Micah is simply saying that instead of dismissing power, or using it unthinkingly, we need to ask the question: how do we reimagine the use of power so that it leads to human flourishing—so that we can use it to help those people who are under-privileged?

Here are a few aspects of the proper use of power:

1. It exposes falsehood, even in our own lives. It takes strength to admit one's weaknesses.

2. It seeks the good of others. Power properly used is willing to embrace personal sacrifice so that others might gain. Conversely, it refuses to sacrifice others for personal gain.

3. It leads to flourishing. It makes all the difference in the world whether or not you're properly using power that can either lead to flourishing or famishing, to restoration or ruin.

These were all evident in Micah's use of power, in contrast to the example of the false prophets.

In his book *The Homeless Mind,* Peter Berger, formerly an emeritus professor at Boston College, talks about how traditional cultures emphasize honor and modern cultures emphasize dignity. In traditional cultures, each person is assigned a role in the community. That's why honor and shame are things that are always imposed by a standard or expectation outside of oneself. These are things that are placed on individuals because they are inherited, depending on where that person comes from and into what position or family they were born. In modern cultures, individuals don't receive their identities based on what their communities assign to them, but rather based on how well they perform and achieve on their own. That's why modern people are prone to pursuing their dreams and being aspirational. Traditional people are less personally aspirational because they want to know what's best for their community.

The point is not that modern people should go back to the traditional ways and be more non-Western; the point is that Micah's identity was neither inherited as in a traditional culture, nor earned as in a modern culture. His identity and role were completely outside of himself, not from the community or through his achievements. The reason why he has what he has, and is who he is, is that something outside of himself has been put into him. That is why Micah says, "But as for me, I am filled with power, with the Spirit of the LORD, and with justice and might" (Micah **3:8**). Power and justice have been infused to his life.

The Greatest Prophet and the Greatest Power

Micah continues in **verse 12**: "Therefore because of you Zion shall be plowed as a field." Because of its leaders' actions, Zion will receive judgment. Is it possible that there can now be any other outcome? Yes. God's warnings of judgment are warnings, right up until the moment the judgment falls. This is the lesson that the people of Nineveh learned when God's prophet Jonah told them, "Yet forty days, and Nineveh shall be overthrown!" (Jonah 3:4). The king commanded repentance in sackcloth, in the hope that, "Who knows? God may turn and relent and turn from his fierce anger, so that we may not perish" (v 9)—which is precisely what God then did (v 10).

Jonah, infamously, was furious at this result (4:1-4). He had hoped his power would be used—and that God's power would be used—in judgment. Micah is different than Jonah—he uses his Spirit-given power to preach truth and warn of God's anger, and he mourns over the coming judgment (Micah 1:8-9), rather than, as Jonah did, over the judgment not coming. Jonah hints negatively, and Micah hints positively, at what Jesus makes clear—that the only thing that transforms power is love. Look at the way parents relate to their infant. They have an incredible amount of power to do good or bad to their child. The infant is utterly dependent upon the parent and at the mercy of how they use their power. Yet most parents learn to use their power in a way that helps their child. That's the only way that power will be transformed. Only love transforms power. Love is the only thing that is more powerful than power and is therefore able to transform it. Imagine seeing a child walking along a sidewalk with a parent, and the child goes out in the street to chase after a ball just as a vehicle comes. It's about to strike the child. There's a split second to push the child to safety, but, despite the risk to their own safety and life, most parents wouldn't even hesitate. If given the choice between sparing the life of their children or their own, they would choose to give up their own lives for the sake of their children. That's the heart impulse of a parent. That's the kind of love that can transform power.

We are meant to look away from and beyond Micah, to the greatest prophet—to Jesus, who, though he was the victim of flagrant abuse of power by both the religious and political leaders of his day, nevertheless properly used his power for the good of others and absorbed the judgment of God in their stead. The Son of Man, the most powerful man in the cosmos, the one who rules everything for all time, did not come to be served, but to use his power to serve others (Mark 10:45). Jesus is the One filled with the Spirit of God who is greater than Micah or Jonah. Compare Jesus with what Micah says of the leaders in Micah **3:9-10**: "Hear this, you heads of the house of Jacob and rulers of the house of Israel, who detest justice and make crooked all that is straight, who build Zion with blood and Jerusalem with iniquity." Jesus built Zion and Jerusalem too, but not with the blood of others; he built with his own blood. He used his power in love.

So the right use of power becomes possible because of him, as we follow him, the only One who had all the power and yet used his power only for his people. That's where true power comes from. It's not that Jesus relinquished his power—only somebody who actually has power can give anything. Jesus

> Right use of power becomes possible because of Jesus.

didn't abandon his power, but he gave up his privilege and his rights. When he died on the cross, he didn't lose his power, but he did give up his privilege. He was still the second person of the Godhead. He could have left the cross, yet he chose to stay on it. He had the power to give his life and die on the cross so that his people would be able to exercise power for its true and proper use: human flourishing and justice—that is, helping those who are less privileged.

Steward Leaders

What does this look like? God's people are called, whenever and how-ever we are called to any leadership, to be steward leaders. To the degree that we have power, rank, and privilege, we have power—but we also, to that same degree, have the responsibility to act as stew-ards. In the ancient world, the steward leader was a servant or slave who also had the power to manage the estate of the owner. That's what God's people are called to do. If we only view our Christian lives as being a calling to be servants, then we're not going to be bold or lead. But timidity doesn't honor God, because he has given us the gifts of any power and privilege that we have, and he wants us to leverage them well. Don't shy away from it. God's people have to be bold and, when called, to lead.

On the other hand, we also need to realize that we must not be domineering and misuse our power and rank by dismissing others. Only when we consider ourselves steward leaders will we be able to be bold and humble at the same time. If we only emphasize the stewardship, we just try to be humble and aren't able to lead. If we only emphasize the leadership part, then we get too bold and be-come abrasive. Only when we understand the gospel of what Jesus has done—how he gave up the privilege of his power, how he used power properly in order to benefit us—are we able to live as steward leaders. "Who then is the faithful and wise manager?" asked Jesus at the beginning of one parable (Luke 12:42-48). It is the one who knows his power has been given him by God, who acknowledges that he has that power, but who remembers that he is given that power in order to serve those who have not been given it, rather than to serve his own pleasures as he forgets that there is a Lord who will hold him to account (v 42-46).

Think about it this week in your work context, in your living situation, in your neighborhood, and in your relationships with family and friends. We have all sorts of power and privilege. Don't misuse it, but equally don't fail to use it at all. Let the gospel inform and shape the way you understand it. Because we follow Jesus, we do not domineer, we do not oppress, we do not live in superiority, but we are able to be humble and bold, to be steward leaders. As a result, we can reflect the beautiful, paradoxical leadership of this greatest King, who gave his life.

Questions for reflection

1. How does, or could, a love for others transform your use of power?

2. How does considering the way Jesus used his power help us neither to misuse our power, nor fail to use it?

3. How does this chapter prompt you to pray for your church leaders?

4. HOPE RESTORED

Micah 4 brings a hopeful shifting of gears to the narrative. There seems to be a lack of hope in the first three chapters, albeit that they showed that God was still present with his people, even in the process of dealing with their idolatrous actions, and with the injustice, oppression, and abuse of power they had caused.

We've seen that, in a way, Micah reflects human experience, because human hearts are in the grip of idolatry. We all have the tendency to be unjust, and our lives are marked by the misuse of power and privilege, and by us using our power for our own personal gain—even at the expense of harming others—rather than leveraging it in order to help others benefit.

It is a challenge to find hope in the midst of all that. The question should be pressing upon us by now: Where is the hope and restoration? Is there realistic hope for our world that extends beyond our own individualistic dreams of comfort, respect, security, and so on? Is there any hope that our world will start spinning in the right direction, or are we bound to destroy ourselves and one another forever?

The Bible argues that, yes, this cosmic hope does exist. But where is the source? In chapter 4, we find that in the midst of all the chaos that has been described in the first three chapters, God injects a vision of astounding hope. He gives us a promise of restoration, a picture of restoration, and, as we look to the New Testament, the experience of restoration.

On His Mountain

In **4:1** we find the promise of restoration: "It shall come to pass in the latter days that the mountain of the house of the LORD shall be established as the highest of the mountains, and it shall be lifted up above the hills, and peoples shall flow to it."

After the first three chapters that discussed the corrupted hearts, actions, and leaders of God's people, Micah promises that in the latter days, God's rule will be established. There is much to unpack here in order to fully appreciate what is being promised. First, "in the latter days" simply means that it will happen in the future. Next, notice that the promise is communicated through this idea of "the mountain of the house of the LORD." When we think about mountains, we usually think about majesty and something that is enormous; something that is very beautiful in its scale. When the Bible talks about mountains, it's not just a geographic reference or a beautiful image; there are deep theological implications for what the biblical writers are intending to say when they make reference to a mountain.

For example, when we see Mount Sinai, where God gave the Law (Exodus 19 – 31), we understand that mountains are where God's rule is established. Here in Micah 4 there is a reference to Mount Zion (the mountain on the side of which Jerusalem had been built), where God dwells in the midst of his people. Mountains are where God rules and where God dwells. So when there is a reference to the mountain of God, you have both the rule and dwelling place of God. We also see this in **verse 2**, which equates the mountain of the LORD with the house of the God of Jacob: "Come, let us go up to the mountain of the LORD, to the house of the God of Jacob." When we read of the house of God, we need to think of the temple of God, which was located in Jerusalem, on Mount Zion—the place where the presence of God dwells.

How do we know that this is what Micah is emphasizing? Because he uses a parallel structure in order to emphasize it. **Verse 2**: "For out of Zion shall go forth the law, and the word of the LORD from

Jerusalem." Often when poets or writers want to emphasize some-thing, they use parallel structures. They use different words referring to the same thing.

Here, Micah inverts that parallel structure—he mentions the places before he speaks of what happens there—in order to provide greater emphasis. The point is that the emphasis is on both where God dwells and also where he rules. We are being asked to think about both the law and the word. Micah is trying to say that if you want to know anything about the promise of restoration, you need to understand it in terms of God's mountain—the place where he dwells and also the place where he rules. The promise of restoration involves both his presence and his rule. God promises to come to his people, and in do-ing so, to make all things right.

The Promise-Maker

We might think that this is just some pie-in-the-sky promise. But in fact, all promises are actually pie in the sky. Every promise is depen-dent upon the promise-maker, and upon whether or not they are trustworthy to carry out that promise. Somebody can make a promise, but the only way you know whether or not that promise is going to be kept—in the midst of all the oppression and injustice—is to know the promise-maker; to know whether or not that promise-maker is trustworthy.

The promise given here in Micah uses similar language to that which we find in Zephaniah 3:14-17:

"Sing, Daughter Zion; shout aloud, Israel! Be glad and rejoice with all your heart, O Daughter Jerusalem! The LORD has taken away your punishment; he has turned back your enemy. The LORD, the King of Israel, is with you; never again will you fear any harm. On that day they will say to Jerusalem, 'Do not fear, Zion; do not let your hands hang limp. The LORD your God is with you, the Mighty Warrior who saves. He will take great delight in you;

in his love he will no longer rebuke you, but will quiet you with his love; he will rejoice over you with singing.'" (NIV)

This is a promise that injects a vision of hope. Ed Welch puts it this way:

> "Nothing delightful about ourselves is being described here. Nothing to sing about, and that is the point. This is not about us, it's about God. He is the One who takes away our punishment. He is the One who gives us new hearts. His singing comes from the work that he has done for us in restoring us ... God simply asks us to come to him with nothing." (*Running Scared,* page 231)

"Come, let us go up to the mountain" (Micah **4:2**). What is God, through Micah, asking us? He's not asking us to bring to him something that we do not have, but to come into what he has done for us. As he says elsewhere, through the prophet Jeremiah,

> "This is the covenant that I will make with the house of Israel after those days, declares the LORD: I will put my law within them, and I will write it on their hearts. And I will be their God, and they shall be my people ... For I will forgive their iniquity, and I will remember their sin no more." (Jeremiah 31:33, 34)

This is the promise of restoration.

Oftentimes when someone makes a promise to us, it is because they have hurt or wronged us: "I promise I won't do that again." "I promise I'll make it up to you." "I promise I'll be good." Parents often hear those phrases from their children. But the difference between this promise-maker and ourselves (and our children) as promise-makers is that when God makes promises to us, it is not because he has done something wrong, but because we have done something wrong. When God promises, he is not doing it because he has wronged us, but because we have wronged him. His past performance does not indicate the promise might not be kept (a feeling many parents experience when their children promise to be good from now on!)—he has done nothing wrong. Further, God's promises are promises freely made by the only **sovereignly** free Person in the universe; he is not at the mercy of circumstances.

To hope in the promise of God is not unreasonable, first, because of his character, and second, because of his power. He is a trustworthy promise-maker.

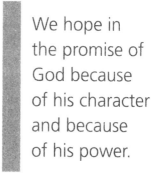

We hope in the promise of God because of his character and because of his power.

A Picture of Restoration

The second thing we see in Micah 4 is the picture of restoration. In Micah 1, we were told that human hearts are twisted by idolatry. What happens when our hearts are drawn to other objects of affection and value and worship? We experience worry, we have anxieties, we despair, and there is hopelessness. We have misplaced hopes in other things. We desire to be set free from the slavery of fear, but we lack the means to set ourselves free. What is the picture of restoration in response to this? Micah promises in **4:2** that "many nations shall come, and say: 'Come, let us go up to the mountain of the LORD, to the house of the God of Jacob, that he may teach us his ways and that we may walk in his paths.' For out of Zion shall go forth the law, and the word of the LORD from Jerusalem." In other words, where the people used to be compelled by idols—by those false gods worshiped at counterfeit shrines on other mountains and high places—the people have now been brought close to God; God will, he promises, dwell among them, and they will walk his way.

In Micah 2 we saw that all human beings are damaged by oppression, violence, war, economic injustice, racism, sexism, and so on. We desire an end to all of the bloodshed and terror. What is the picture of restoration in response to this? It comes in **4:3**: "He shall judge between many peoples, and shall decide disputes for strong nations far away; and they shall beat their swords into **plowshares**, and their spears into pruning hooks; nation shall not lift up sword against nation, neither shall they learn war anymore." "Many peoples" and "strong nations far away" will be brought together; God will bring justice. Swords will be turned into plowshares; in other words, instruments of violence will become instruments of the vineyard. What was once used to destroy and bring death will now be used to plant and sustain life. That which was a picture of death will be renewed and restored to produce the reality of life. There will be no need for conflict; no one will need or want to "learn war anymore."

As modern readers, we can easily miss some of the different things that are going on here. The language used here in Micah 4 is similar to the language in chapter 1. Micah uses the same language in both chapters and there are several similar parallels.

1. 1:3—"The LORD ... will ... tread upon the high places."

2. **4:2**—"The house of the LORD shall be established as the highest of the mountains."

1. 1:4—"The mountains will melt under him."

2. **4:2**—"The mountain of the LORD."

1. 1:7—"Carved images shall be beaten to pieces."

2. **4:3**—"They shall beat their swords into plowshares."

The reason why the prophet is doing this is because he is saying that God's solution—restoration—is not evacuation. God's solution for the injustice, oppression, idolatry, and the misuse of power is not to simply evacuate his people from those experiences. Therefore, when we think about restoration and even the new heavens and new earth as the place of ultimate and eternal restoration, we need to realize that it's not as though God just takes us away and brings us into some other location. No, he renews the old earth into a new earth. It's a restoration, renewal, and renovation of everything we know.

In chapter 1, Micah talked about the sin of the daughter of Zion, but now in chapter 4 he talks about how in Zion the law will go forth. There are references to Jerusalem in both chapters; there are references to war and to shame and fear in both chapters. The point here is that Micah is saying that this restoration will break into the midst of all the brokenness and fallenness we experience every day.

Sometimes there is a longing in every heart that says, *God, just come with a wrecking crew and destroy it all. Can you just get rid of my terrible circumstances? I'm overwhelmed and depressed and anxious. Just take me out of all this!* But God is going to do things differently, and better, than that. He says, *In the midst of your broken-ness and fallenness, I'm going to restore.* That helps us to understand what he is promising. This is a picture of a life in this world, but made perfect—this existence, but renewed, and enjoyed for all eternity.

We first moved into our home almost 10 years ago. It's an old home (by American standards!), built around 1865. And there was a lot of work that needed to be done. There were some old windows that had been there for probably 60 or 70 years that needed to be replaced right away—so we decided to get some replacement windows. Now, imagine if the carpenter came in with all sorts of heavy machinery. No—that's not the way you restore something. You repair something delicately. You restore it carefully. When somebody comes to repair an old home, they are going to make sure that the beautiful, original moldings from the windows are preserved. They have to be very delicate.

That's exactly how God surgically restores our lives, and will one day restore his world. He's taking down those weapons that were used, and he doesn't just discard them. Instead he transforms and restores them as instruments of life. At one point they were instruments of death, but he restores and transforms them. That's what he does with our lives. He takes all of the things in our life that seem as though they will break down our life, and by his grace, he can restore them. God cares; he doesn't just discard and get rid of things. He renews them.

Questions for reflection

1. How are God's promises different than ours? What do we lose if we forget these differences?

2. What aspect of this picture of restoration most thrills you, and why?

3. God "doesn't just discard and get rid of things. He renews them." Can you see how God is doing this in your own life? Can you look back on times when he has done this for you in the past?

PART TWO

We can look to more mountains than Old Testament Mount Zion to give us confidence that we will experience restoration.

When we look through the Bible, we see the idea of the mountain of the Lord and Mount Zion being developed, and we encounter something very interesting in Hebrews 12. The author of Hebrews was writing to a Jewish Christian community who were under a great amount of persecution and were experiencing the temptation to abandon their Christian faith in order to find some level of protection under Judaism. That's the situation the writer speaks into. And here is what he writes in Hebrews 12:22-24:

> "But you have come to Mount Zion and to the city of the living God, the heavenly Jerusalem, and to innumerable angels in festal gathering, and to the assembly of the firstborn who are enrolled in heaven, and to God, the judge of all, and to the spirits of the righteous made perfect, and to Jesus, the **mediator** of a new covenant."

The writer is using Mount Zion as a reference to—a shadow of—Jesus. Jesus is the fulfillment of the promise made about how he will rule and dwell from Jerusalem, and give to his people his law and his word. His rule and his dwelling are now fulfilled in the person of Jesus. "But you have come to Mount Zion ... and to Jesus, the mediator of a new covenant."

But this sets up a tension in our experience. That tension is that we've come to Mount Zion, to Jesus, to the great restored city. But, at the same time, we still experience brokenness and fallenness, oppression and injustice, and expressions of idolatry—not only or even primarily around us, but right here in our own hearts. How does this get reconciled? How is the tension resolved?

The answer is: by the Lord Jesus, on Mount Zion.

Only the Shadow

In *Walking With God Through Pain and Suffering*, Tim Keller tells the story of a famous preacher at Tenth Presbyterian Church in Philadelphia in the first half of the twentieth century. His name was Dr. Donald Gray Barnhouse, and his wife died when their daughter was still young. He wanted to come up with a good illustration to explain to his young daughter what had happened to his wife, her mother. One day as he was in the car with his daughter, a huge truck passed by them, and the shadow of the truck swept over the car. Dr. Barnhouse asked the little girl, "If you were to get hit by the truck, would you prefer that you get hit by the truck itself, or get hit by the shadow of the truck?"

She answered, "Oh daddy! The shadow of the truck rather than the truck itself because it won't hurt as much."

He responded along these lines: "That's exactly what happened to your mother. The shadow of the truck of the judgment of death came over your mother, but she is still alive. She's actually more alive than we are. She's in the presence of God, and we will see her someday. You need to understand that only the shadow of the judgment of death went over her, but the truck of the judgment of death crushed Jesus. The crushing judgment of the truck ran over Jesus so only the shadow will go over us, your mother, and all who place their faith in him" (*Walking with God through Pain and Suffering*, page 317).

We may ask: *Do we have evidence that God is going to keep his promise that we will dwell under his rule?* Of course we do! God's Son hung on a cross at Calvary on the side of Mount Zion. There is an empty tomb on the side of that same mountain. This is what Jesus accomplished through his life, death, and resurrection. His resurrection is the receipt of his payment, and the payment is what has canceled the debt that our idolatry, injustice and oppression have incurred.

At the Peak and at the Foot

The restoration that Christ's death and resurrection have won was anticipated in two wonderful episodes, one at the peak of another mountain, and the other at its foot.

"After six days Jesus took with him Peter and James and John, and led them up a high mountain by themselves. And he was transfigured before them, and his clothes became radiant, intensely white, as no one on earth could bleach them." (Mark 9:2-3)

This is a picture of the glory, the majesty, and the presence of God. Then Elijah and Moses come down. How does Peter respond? "Let us make three tents, one for you and one for Moses and one for Elijah" (v 5). He sensed that there was, as there always had been since Eden, a gap between the glory and holiness of God on the one hand, and those who are sinners on the other. This was why at Mount Sinai in Exodus 25 – 31, God had given instructions to his people to build the tabernacle: the tent where his presence would reside. It would be a place where God would meet with his people. The tabernacle spoke both of God's presence and God's unapproachable holiness. And on the mount of transfiguration Peter sees the glorious holiness of Jesus and says, *We need a tabernacle*. But he never builds one. Why? Because in the coming of God as incarnate flesh, that God-man both *is* the tabernacle (he is where we meet with God) and *removes our need for* the tabernacle (he is how the glorious God becomes approachable).

Then later on after they come down the mountain, there is a man who comes and brings his son, who is possessed by a demon. Jesus asks how long the boy has been so afflicted, and his father answers:

"'From childhood. And it has often cast him into fire and into water, to destroy him. But if you can do anything, have compassion on us and help us.'

"And Jesus said to him, '"If you can"! All things are possible for one who believes.' Immediately the father of the child cried out and said, 'I believe; help my unbelief!' And when Jesus saw that

Micah 4 v 1-5

a crowd came running together, he rebuked the unclean spirit, saying to it, 'You mute and deaf spirit, I command you, come out of him and never enter him again.' And after crying out and convulsing him terribly, it came out, and the boy was like a corpse, so that most of them said, 'He is dead.' But Jesus took him by the hand and lifted him up, and he arose.

"And when he had entered the house, his disciples asked him privately, 'Why could we not cast it out?' And he said to them, 'This kind cannot be driven out by anything but prayer.'"

(Mark 9:21-29)

The disciples can't cast out the demon in this young boy, and they cannot understand why. Jesus responds by saying that there are certain things that you cannot do without prayer. The disciples were underestimating the power of evil. They thought they could handle it themselves and restore the boy in their own strength. The boy's father didn't make the same mistake. He said, "I believe; help my unbelief!" He didn't say, *I have enough righteousness and faith and everything that is required for you to properly respond to my need.* Instead he said, *I have absolutely nothing. There's nothing that I can bring before you. I have no righteousness on my own. I can't help my son, so can you please help him even though I don't have enough belief? I have doubts, but I have enough belief in you and little enough in myself to have brought him to you.*

Keller puts it this way: "Through Jesus we don't need perfect righteousness, just repentant helplessness" (*Kings Cross*, page 121). When we ask God for help and want to experience restoration, God doesn't say to us, *I want you to have perfect righteousness. Work it up and then I'll help you;* nor does he say, *Do everything that you can to make the situation right, and then I will help you.* If you can help yourself, why would you need God to restore you?

> God doesn't say to us, *Do everything you can, and then I will help you.*

70

God wants somebody who has a repentant helplessness, not a perfect righteousness.

Here is the point: the One who was transfigured on that mountain is also the One who died on Mount Zion to take the judgment for our lack of righteousness. He took the punishment for our idolatry. The cross is where "the house of the LORD"—the presence of God in human form—was "lifted up" (Micah **4:1**). And so his holy presence can dwell among us, and within us, to help and transform and restore our hopeless situations as we come to him and say, *God, I have nothing to give, and I cannot do this myself. Even my belief is weak, but I'm here, coming to you for help.*

Hope Changes All

Keller tells a further story in *Walking With God Through Pain and Suffering,* about two men who were both convicted of serious crimes and given long sentences. As they began their time in prison, one prisoner was told that his wife and son had died. The other knew that his wife and daughter were still alive. How do you think that affected their experience while they were in prison? The guy who heard the news that his wife and son had died, after about two years of wasting away, ultimately died in prison. The other prisoner, who knew that his wife and daughter were still alive, endured the harsh conditions of the prison and was freed ten years later to be reunited to his family (page 314).

Here's the principle: what you know to be true of the future will inform your experience now. What you know of your future will inform the way you endure all the suffering, oppression, and injustice of this life. We will be able to endure if we know that God has already, in Jesus, brought about restoration, and so he is restoring us now in all the circumstances of our lives (Romans 8:28), and he will one day fully restore us. We will be able to experience all of the harsh conditions of the dungeon while we're living here on earth with the knowledge that the promise-maker is also the one who is a promise-keeper.

This is the great injection of hope that Micah 4 brings, which would sustain God's people through their time in exile. And this is the great injection of hope that Micah 4, read this side of the cross, brings us as we struggle with the complexities and disappointments and griefs of this life—some self-inflicted, and others at the hands of others. Jesus has absorbed all the injustice and oppression and death. Only the shadow goes over us as we experience the fallenness of this world. That is what we experience; so we can know that we can have the real experience of restoration now in part, and one day fully. Death is already overcome, it has lost its sting, and it can no longer make us ultimately afraid (Micah **4:4**). God walks with us and dwells in us by his Spirit now, and will come to dwell with us in all his fullness one day. He continues to tell us that this is not our final experience in life. There is ultimate hope because death hit Jesus so that we would only get the shadow. This is how we know we can "walk in the name of the LORD our God forever and ever" (**v 5**).

Questions for reflection

1. How are you experiencing the tension between having come to "Mount Zion … the heavenly Jerusalem" and having to live in this fallen world?

2. How has this section shaped and enlarged your view of the Lord Jesus?

3. "God wants somebody who has a repentant helplessness, not a perfect righteousness." Who needs to hear this truth from you today? (Maybe the answer is, "I do"!)

5. THE LONG ROAD TO RESTORATION

How are we going to be able to get from the brokenness and fallenness that we experience, to the future that has been described and that God's people will one day enjoy? In the next two chapters of this book, we will assess how to address the in-between period, from where we are to where we are going.

This chapter is entitled "The Long Road to Restoration" because God does not offer us shortcuts. Most of us know that with anything beautiful and valuable in life there is a path we need to walk to reach it. There are no shortcuts. I'm always looking for shortcuts to become fit and remain healthy. I think through all the possible answers and then (reluctantly) I conclude that there is no easy way to get there. I'm going to have to move my body and engage in physical activity.

The road to restoration is long, narrow, and hard. In this chapter we're going to look at three signposts on this long road to restoration.

First, we'll look at restoration *from* pain. If there's going to be restoration, we would expect to be restored from pain and suffering. Second, we'll consider restoration *through* pain. This might be more surprising to you since as Westerners we love restoration from pain, but not so much restoration through pain. Then lastly, we'll look at the perspective restoration gives us *in* our pain.

Restoration from Pain

As we have seen, the Israelites were under much oppression, and they were also perpetrators of much oppression. There was injustice; their leaders were misusing their power, and manipulating and exploiting the marginalized. This is the picture of what was going on. They were suffering under immense pain in trials, some of that because of their own idolatry. But (as we saw in the last chapter) God wanted them to know that the way things were was not how things would always be. We tend to look at what we have now and work things out from there; but how things are right now is not the way that God wants the world to be—so he shows us what we as his people will enjoy one day, and invites us to work things out from there. And the headline to remember is: we will be restored from pain.

Here's a little **apologetic** sidebar about pain. True Christianity is a faith that differs from all the typical approaches to pain. Some want to deny that pain exists. Others of us face life with an ungrounded optimism that our pain is going to go away. Sometimes people tell me that the problem of pain and suffering is Christianity's number one problem because Christianity, according to some people, doesn't seem to have an answer to the problem of pain. My first response usually is that the problem of pain is not simply a problem of Christianity. I'll agree with them that it is problematic; it's not easy, and there is no simple explanation for it. But the problem of pain is a problem for every human individual, for every life and for every worldview. Every system must provide a credible, reasonable response to the problem of pain. It's not just a problem for Christianity; it's a problem for humanism, atheism, **eastern mysticism**, and **agnosticism**. Pain is a problem for everyone, because the experience of pain is universal.

> True Christianity differs from all the typical approaches to pain.

And the impulse to avoid pain is almost as universal. What do we often long for and daydream about? It is typically attached to some form of pain avoidance. People say or think, "There is so much suffering and hardship right now—a lot of trials and difficult people and circumstances—and I long for a day, a moment or week, when these things will be taken away." We long for a day when pain can be avoided.

Do you long for financial security? The reason why you long for financial security is because you want to avoid the tension and stress of financial insecurity. You long to avoid the physical pain of discomfort, or you long to avoid the societal pain of your positional loss or low status. Perhaps you long for a satisfying love relationship. You might yearn for this because you want to avoid the mental pain of bearing the weight of life all on your own. You don't want to be lonely. You don't want to be alone. You want to avoid the disappointments that people have expressed to and about you about you being single.

These longings are not problematic in themselves; they are desperate attempts to overcome pain within ourselves. We do not want pain in our lives. The Bible, of course, provides an honest assessment of the experience of pain. Look at the promise in Micah **4:6-7** that one day things will be made right: "I will assemble the lame and gather those who have been driven away and those whom I have afflicted; and the lame I will make the remnant, and those who were cast off, a strong nation; and the LORD will reign over them in Mount Zion from this time forth and forevermore." There are two groups of people that are being addressed: the lame (representing the pain caused by brokenness inside of us) and those who are cast off (representing the pain caused by the brokenness of circumstances outside of us). Whether our pain comes from inside or outside of us, God promises to restore us from all of it.

Just by looking at people on the surface, we can't usually tell whether or not there's a lot of pain in their lives. We are pain-avoiders, and we also tend to be pain-hiders. A person might be going through all sorts of hurt, tension, fear, anxiety, and stress. They look fine, but they're like a duck on a pond, which looks completely composed above the water, but underneath they're kicking their feet. The insides of our lives are often in turmoil. And right in the middle of all that, God injects a vision of hope. He promises to restore us from the pain that is in our hearts and the pain that is outside of us. The lame will become the remnant God saves, and the cast-off people will be made strong (**v 7**).

Jacob's Limp

I think that there is an implicit reference to Genesis 32:22-32 here, because here the word "lame" is not the typical word used for lame such as we find in the new-creational passages in the book of Isaiah (Isaiah 35:6), which are picked up later on in Jesus' own ministry (John 5:3). The word that is used here is alluding back to Jacob when he was wrestling with God in Genesis 32. Before we go to that scene, let me set the background. Jacob had been running away from God, his brother Esau, his father Isaac, and ultimately from himself and his difficult life circumstances.

In Genesis 25:28 it says, "Isaac loved Esau..." It doesn't say that Isaac loved Esau and loved his other son, Jacob, as well. It simply says that Jacob's father loved his older brother. Could you imagine growing up in a household where you knew that your father loved your sibling but that he didn't really love you for whatever reason? A life of never quite measuring up to his expectations and standards. A childhood where your father was always prouder of your older twin brother because he was better in school, or more athletic, or more musically talented, or perhaps better looking, or whatever. Whatever the reasons might be, one of your parents favored your older or younger sibling, but somehow that favor was elusive for you.

This is what it says about Jacob. But Jacob ended up stealing his brother's **birthright**—the blessing God had promised his grandfather Abraham, which Abraham had passed on to Isaac, and which Isaac meant to pass to Esau but was duped into passing to Jacob. Genesis 27:41 tells us that (unsurprisingly) "Esau hated Jacob." Jacob is rejected by his father; his older brother hates him and wants to kill him. The only person who favors Jacob is his mother, but his mother dies. He becomes a wanderer. He runs away. It takes years for him to go back. In the midst of those circumstances, God meets him in Genesis 32:24-30, where he wrestles with God. God comes in the form of a man and wrestles with him, and touches his hip socket, and Jacob becomes injured in a way that causes him to limp; yet at the same time Jacob receives God's blessing. For the rest of his life, he would have a limp to his step, and he would always be reminded that the limp had happened because he wrestled with God, but he now knew what it was to be blessed by God.

The thing here is that the limp was not God's punishment. The limp was remedial. It was a means by which Jacob would recall this experience of knowing that God was with him and had restored him, even though his name meant, "he cheats." Here was somebody who was a wanderer and running away from God, and yet God met him and restored him from his pain, even though he had been given a limp. Jacob's pain was caused in part by circumstances and in part by his response to those circumstances. But God restores the lame. And Micah uses the same word that described Jacob's lameness, so that God's people in his day would know that this was how God would deal with them, too. They may have been lame, but they were also blessed—and only the second would last.

Exile, Then Rescue

This brings us to our second point: not only does God restore us from pain, but he also restores us through pain. God tells his people that there will be pain, comparing their present trials to a "woman in labor" (Micah **4:9**), and then pointing them forward to a future no less difficult: "Writhe and groan, O daughter of Zion, like a woman in labor, for now you shall go out from the city and dwell in the open country; you shall go to Babylon" (**v 10**). But there will then come restoration: "There you shall be rescued; there the LORD will redeem you from the hand of your enemies."

The emphasis is on "There you shall be rescued; there the LORD will redeem you." "There" is referring to Babylon. God says that he will restore them. In verse 4 Micah promised that God's people "shall sit every man under his vine and under his fig tree, and no one shall make them afraid." There is this promise of restoration, but God says that it will be not only from pain, but through pain. God says in effect in **verses 10-12**, *You're going to go into exile and captivity. There will be another nation that will come and oppress you. You will live in exile away from Jerusalem, where the temple and presence of God are found. Your enemies will seek to take you over. But I will not leave you abandoned.*

The **analogy** of labor is well chosen. After all, what is one kind of pain that around half of the human race, in the vast majority of cases, willingly accepts? The pain of childbirth. At the time of writing this, our youngest will turn 14 in a month, so it's been a long time—but I still remember (albeit not as well as my wife, I'm sure!) the day when each of our children was born. If you've seen that or gone through it, that's a very, very challenging period. But it's also wonderful. A woman labors through the pain of childbirth because on the other side of it… there is new life. And (usually straightaway, though sometimes it can take time) a mother wants to see and hold her child, despite all the pain—because she has been blessed through that pain.

The kind of restoration the Bible is talking about happens through pain. Micah uses the metaphor of the agony and pain of childbirth to help us to understand the way in which our restoration is going to happen. He talks about impending exile in Babylon. God shows them the bed of affliction that they have made—but he is gracious enough to rescue them from having to ultimately and eternally sleep in it. He says, *You're going to go through pain. There will be suffering, but I'm not ultimately going to leave you there; restoration is going to come through that.* Restoration from pain comes via a path through pain.

Questions for reflection

1. How do you tend to deal with the existence of pain in your life? Do you think those reactions are helpful, unhelpful, or a mixture?

2. God's people were both lame and blessed. How is this the case for you? And how does it change your perspective to know that for the Christian, only the second will last?

3. How does the analogy of a woman in labor help you to view your pain, or the pain of those you love, today?

PART TWO

Finding the Meaning

Peter Berger has said that, "Every worldview, every culture, every individual wants to find meaning in the experience of suffering and pain" (from Keller, *Walking With God Through Pain and Suffering*, page 163—and some of the argument that follows is based on this book). Everyone wants some sort of explanation.

Here's part of the Bible's explanation. God will not evacuate his people from pain; but he will restore us through pain. That's what the Bible wants to tell us. Even though there is a lot of pain, we know that pain and suffering provide purpose and meaning. The ancients referred to this when they talked about "the usefulness of suffering."

Jonathan Haidt, a **moral psychologist**, says:

"People need adversity, setbacks, and perhaps even trauma to reach the highest levels of strength, fulfillment, and personal development." (*The Happiness Hypothesis*, page 136)

He then tells the story of a young man, whom he calls Greg. Greg's wife committed adultery and left the marriage to live with another man. She took their two young children, and Greg had to fight for custody of his own children. He was a junior professor at a college and wasn't earning a lot of money. He went through a lot of stress, heartache, and hardship, but he ultimately won custody of his children. However, he had a full-time job so he wasn't able to care for them as well as he would have liked.

Haidt, the psychologist, was a friend of Greg and when he visited him, he discovered something quite remarkable. Through Greg's adverse circumstances, other people in his community and his church came alongside of him and started to support, love, and pray for him. His parents, who lived 1000 miles away, decided to temporarily transplant themselves to live in his area in order to help him care for his children. Haidt commented that "something very, very powerful happened when I was speaking with him, and I choked up when that happened." He describes it thus:

"When you go to an opera, there is usually a very, very important moment in the opera where there is an aria, where there is a sad and moving solo. At that moment, what ends happening is that the story changes through that aria as the solo is being performed. The narrative changes from sorrow into something very amazing and beautiful. [Greg said to Haidt] 'This is my moment to sing the aria. I don't want to. I don't want to have this chance, but it's here now, and what am I going to do about it? Am I going to rise to the occasion?'"

(*The Happiness Hypothesis*, page 136)

Greg "sang the aria." And so he was able to have his entire perspective changed; everything else in his life got transformed in light of his suffering and pain. Greg, Haidt goes on to say, had found himself...

"... reacting to others with much greater sympathy, love, and forgiveness. He just couldn't get mad at people for little things anymore." (*The Happiness Hypothesis*, page 138)

The petty things had become petty to him. He was not troubled by these things because he was someone who had gone through a lot of pain, suffering, hurt, and rejection. Haidt goes on to say that there are three life lessons or "benefits" of suffering—your resilience grows, your relationships become stronger, and your priorities are honed.

Social commentators have said that there are four major categories of goals that shape how we live our lives: namely, personal happiness, relationships, spirituality, and how we pursue the common good for the betterment of our society. These thinkers say that when we just pursue our own personal achievement and happiness, we have

> When we just pursue our happiness, we cannot accommodate adversity without despairing.

no space in our lives to accommodate adversity without despairing. We don't know what to do when adversity visits. In all of the other categories, our goals get enhanced and enriched when we walk through times of adversity; but not when we're merely pursuing our own personal happiness. If all that matters is my happiness, when something even slightly difficult happens, I will crumble and fall apart over little, petty things. I will be unable to have any perspective. Think about all the times when you grumble and whine about little, petty things. Ultimately, it's because you are focused on pursuing personal achievement and happiness. That is why when adversity comes, it's crushing. We don't know what to do with it. So we need to learn to see life as something broader and grander than simply a vehicle for achieving happiness right now. We need to learn that sometimes we must rise to the occasion, and sing the aria, and find that restoration often comes through pain, just as it does in the labor room, and just as it did for God's people in Micah's day, and does still in ours. Happiness is something that is given to us as a gift from God, but oftentimes real happiness and restoration and hope come, and are strengthened, through pain before we ever experience restoration from pain.

The Perspective Pain Brings

The final theme Micah touches on in this section is the perspective that restoration gives us during pain. **Verse 13** gives us a picture of a God who stands by the suffering Israelites and tells them to be strong, for he is indeed with them to bring hope and victory to them. Even before this, **verse 8** told us that this restoration would come through kingship for the Israelites: "Zion, to you shall it come, the former dominion shall come, kingship for the daughter of Jerusalem." God is promising a shalom-enacting kingship. Jesus would come to fulfill this promise: "He will be great and will be called the Son of the Most High. And the Lord God will give to him the throne of his father David, and he will reign over the house of Jacob forever, and of his kingdom there will be no end" (Luke 1:32-33).

But the twist to the plot was the cross. Jesus didn't simply come to enact a shalomic-like state where he would fulfill the promises of restoration forever. He came to experience the judgment of exile. That is how he restores us. On the cross, he experienced the exile of separation from God's blessing and loving presence that you and I deserve, so that we might receive the homecoming that Jesus deserved. God is not unfamiliar with your pain. We also need to know that restoration from pain is utterly and ultimately certain.

The biblical principle is this: the world will give us trials, suffering, and pain. But God packages the pain, hurt, and trials, and he takes us through the trials, not evacuating us from the trials, but seeing us through the trials in order to restore us.

I've lived life long enough to know this principle is true. There have been setbacks, failures, rejections, hurt, abandonment, separation, marginalization, racism, and oppression. I've experienced all those things, and I'm sure you have experienced some of that, or worse than that, as well. But one thing I know for sure is that God did not evacuate me from those circumstances because he wanted to lead me through the circumstances that he might teach me through those circumstances. He restored me through the pain because "suffering produces endurance, and endurance produces character, and character produces hope" (Romans 5:3-4). If we don't know how God uses this, if we reject and want to avoid and deny all the pain in our lives, then we will remain shallow and superficial. Why? Because we're not allowing an important, useful remedial tool that God will use to build us, refine us, and restore us to be the kind of people that we can be.

A Bruised Reed He Will Not Break

There is a wonderful passage in Isaiah 42 that talks about the suffering servant, the Messiah: "A bruised reed he will not break, and a faintly burning wick he will not quench" (Isaiah 42:3). What does this mean? The Hebrew word for "bruised" is not just a little bruise on your leg.

> Our Lord Jesus does not break the bruised reed. He's gentle with it.

It's actually talking about a heavy **contusion**, traumatic to the point where it could be fatal if you receive that kind of a bruise or blow. So this is a reed so broken that it is on the verge of snapping; and the Messiah, our Lord Jesus, does not break that bruised reed. He's very gentle with it. Likewise, imagine looking at a smoldering wick that's about to die and have the light snuffed out of it—but then someone comes along and doesn't just blow it out because he thinks there is no use for it; rather, he fans it back to flame. Jesus cares for those people who are marginalized and hopeless—people who are fragile, hurt, and wounded. People like us, who might be going through a lot of pain. Jesus doesn't take that which is beaten, battered, and bruised, and discard it. He doesn't do that; he doesn't know how to do that. He is a gentle Savior who will restore through pain, but who will never allow that pain to break us.

At one point in J.R.R. Tolkien's *Lord of the Rings,* Gollum is struggling with his own personality, but is clinging to the hope that he could be transformed back into a hobbit all over again and restored from his pain. But Samwise Gamgee comes into the scene and pushes that hope away, and, it says, hope left Smeagol forever. Jesus doesn't enter into our lives to give us pain that will break us or snuff us out. He comes to restore us. The road will likely be long and narrow and oftentimes uphill, but it is a road to restoration, marked out by the Lord of restoration.

God wants us to look at our pain, suffering, and experience in a completely different way. If we do, we'll wake up in the morning giving thanks to God, and we'll go on doing so throughout the day, whatever the day brings our way. We'll wake up knowing there's a purpose and meaning for why each aspect of our life is happening to us: the good and bad, the chosen and unchosen. Rather than saying, "What's the point?" or "I don't know why I bother" and rather than being anxious, we'll live with hope, knowing that restoration lies beyond our pain and comes through our pain. That's the perspective Micah is teaching God's people. Pain and suffering are not a sign of the absence of God. They are a place in which to experience the presence of God because he wants to restore us through them:

"You shall go to Babylon.

[But] There you shall be rescued;

there the LORD will redeem you

from the hand of your enemies." (Micah **4:10**)

Questions for reflection

1. Have you experienced a time of suffering from which you can see how God used it to build you, refine you, or restore you?

2. "Pain and suffering are not a sign of the absence of God. They are a place in which to experience the presence of God." How does this transform our view of difficult times?

3. Do you know a fellow Christian who is "singing the aria" right now—who is a bruised reed? How will you point them to Jesus in order to encourage them?

6. HE SHALL STAND AND SHEPHERD

In the last chapters, we looked at God's vision of hope for his people. Restoration will come, but it is a restoration that will come through the pain of defeat and exile.

The focus in chapter five is not primarily on the theme of restoration, but on the restorer. When a leader announces a grand plan for overhauling anything—an organization, company, or institution—there are certain expectations that arise. And there are particular questions: often most importantly, how will this happen and who will make this happen? Consider all of the wonderful qualities of an effective and fruitful leader. What characteristics come to mind? One would hope that this individual would be able to get a good read on what's happening with the community: somebody who has an ear to the ground. This person might also be somebody who is creative and can effect change, maybe sometimes in unpredictable ways. It would likely be someone with the ability and authority to accomplish and execute the changes that he or she would like to bring about.

What we find here in this section is a picture of the kind of restorer that God's people actually need: the kind of restorer that God is going to send in order to bring about restoration for his people. There are three broad characteristics of this restorer that we find here:

- The restorer is sympathetic.

- The restorer is unexpected.

- The restorer is strong and majestic.

The Restorer Is Sympathetic

First, the restorer is sympathetic. He cares about mankind's plight. He actually cares about humanity's struggles and situations, such as the hardships the Israelites were experiencing.

And here is what Judah would experience when the Assyrian King Sennacherib launched his campaign against God's people. Here is Sennacherib's account:

"But as for [King] Hezekiah, the Jew who did not bow in submission to my yoke, of his strong walled towns and innumerable small villages and their neighborhood I besieged and conquered by stamping down earth ramps and then by bringing up battering rams, by the assault of foot soldiers, by breeches, by tunneling, by sapper operations. I made to come out from them 200,150 people, young and old, male and female, innumerable horses, mules, donkeys, camels, large and small cattle, and counted them as spoils of war."

(Taken from David Alexander and Pat Alexander,
Eerdmans Handbook to the Bible, page 1983)

One can read any of the **annals** of one particular empire conquering another one, but this is typically what happens with all sorts of atrocities and injustices. The Assyrian king counted all of these things as spoils of war.

The questions that the Israelites would surely ask, and that we in our modern context would ask in such dire circumstances, are: *Is God here? Does he care? Is he actually going to do something about this? Is he going to rescue and deliver us?* Naturally, we would question his care for us. *How will he deliver? Will God deliver the way I would like him to? Is our God sympathetic?*

It is into this future disaster that Micah speaks: "Now muster your troops, O daughter of troops; siege is laid against us; with a rod they strike the judge of Israel on the cheek" (**v 1**). God was not oblivious to what was happening to his people then, nor is he oblivious to what is happening in our lives today. He is near to us, despite how distant we often think he is. He was fully aware that the Assyrians would take his people captive. He knew that they didn't have a whole lot of troops. So when Micah says, "O daughter of troops," it seems to be a way of God acknowledging their weakness and inability to fight back and protect their land and people. God has a strong sense of what's going on. He knows. He's not far off and distant. God understands that there will be a small remnant of people—a daughter of troops.

Micah also foretells the powerlessness of Hezekiah, the king of Judah who would be completely at the power of the Assyrian empire. In **verse 1**, the enemy has come so close to the king (the "judge") that they are able to strike him on the cheek. This is an act that would bring great shame on him. He is, in a sense, defenseless to the attacks that have come upon him. But God sees and knows. Even in the moment of shame and utter humiliation, God is sympathetic to his predicament in this dire scenario. God understands. He is present. He knows of their circumstances and conditions.

Oftentimes when we are in distress, we want to know that our needs are heard and recognized. All of us experience something of an **existential** struggle within our own hearts. On the one hand, we want people to know us well—to be aware of our condition. We want people to know that we have needs—whether emotional, physical, social, psychological, or spiritual needs. And we want others to help us in those needs. But on the other hand, we don't want people to truly know us. We want to be known in the sense that we want to be acknowledged or recognized. We want to know that we're valuable and important, that we have dignity, and that our lives have meaning and purpose. So we don't necessarily want people to dismiss or ignore us; yet at the same time, we don't want them to know us *too* well. If they know us too well or too much, then we will be utterly exposed.

> We want people to know us well—but we don't want people to know us *too* well.

If someone knows our worst, they are unlikely to still respect us or to love us. We don't want that, so we seek to present ourselves in a certain way. To a greater or lesser extent, we want people to think that we are perhaps someone that we actually are not.

That is why the existentialist philosopher Jean-Paul Sartre said, "Hell is other people." Granted, this is not a full-orbed definition of what the Bible says about hell, but it makes sense to some degree. Sartre, in his essay "No Exit," depicted hell as a room full of people who have no eyelids. They are perpetually staring into your soul. If you were to look over right now to your neighbor, and look them straight in the eye for approximately 30 seconds, you probably wouldn't be able to hold their gaze. You don't want to feel they are observing you closely with all of your flaws and blemishes—and that's just the visible ones. Surveys suggest that 95% of people would feel utterly uncomfortable being naked in public—but 100% of us feel uncomfortable with being emotionally and spiritually naked.

So we want to be known, valued, and recognized at some level; yet at the same time, we don't want to be known fully. But God wants us to know today that he is fully aware of our situation—that he knows the things we are most embarrassed about and are taking most care to hide from those whose approval we desire. He knows those things, but he still cares and he still loves. He doesn't stare directly into our eyes and crush us because of our blemishes. He looks, he sees, and he sends (or rather, has sent) a restorer who delivers and frees us.

Deeply Known and Deeply Cared For

We need to remember that this prophecy of near-defeat and restoration comes in Micah 5—and the focus of the first three chapters was not on the Assyrian threat, but rather on the idolatry of the people and its effects on their neighbors. In other words, even as Sennacherib lays siege to Jerusalem and strikes the judge/king of Israel on the cheek, Micah wants to say, *This is a problem. But it is not your biggest problem.* The people will need God to provide a restorer, just as he promises to provide one in **verse 2**. But the "one who is to be ruler in Israel" will be one who, in order to bring "peace" (**v 5**), will need to rescue the people not so much from Sennacherib as from themselves. And God cares enough to see not just what his people say they need, but what they really, truly need. He knows. He knows better than us.

On a personal level, this being deeply known and being deeply cared for can be seen beautifully in Luke 5:17-26, where Jesus interacts with a person who is physically disabled. A group of friends take their friend, who is paralyzed, to Jesus. He is unable to walk, so his friends transport him on a mat to Jesus. They believe that Jesus has the power to heal their friend. They arrive at the house where Jesus is teaching, and it's crowded. It's so crowded that they're unable to get in. So they disassemble the tiles on the flat roof and lower their friend down to Jesus.

At that very moment, everything stops. The people in the room shift their attention to this odd spectacle and wonder what Jesus will do next. In Luke 5:20, Jesus says to the paralyzed man, "Man, your sins are forgiven you." This sounds like a very religious thing to say. But the guy didn't come for his sins to be forgiven! He came with different needs. I wonder if he was thinking that Jesus had the wrong guy. He had just been lowered on a mat from the ceiling because of his physical disabilities. He had acute immediate needs and he was asking Jesus to help take care of them.

But Jesus sees more than the man and his friends have seen. Jesus understands this man's plight and knows what his deepest needs are. The ultimate problem in this man's life is not his paralysis. And the main problem in your life is not your suffering or your circumstances. It's not that God doesn't care about your suffering or that he minimizes your pain; but he knows they are not your main problem. The main problem in your life is sin. Because Jesus knows us and because he knows what our needs are, he will address the bigger problem first. "Man, your sins are forgiven you."

How would you complete this sentence? *If only God would come and give _____ to me.* The truth is that whatever you fill in the blank is your counterfeit god. That is where you have placed your hope. *If only God will resolve this, then I will be happy. If only God would take care of this or provide this for me, then I would have so much meaning and security in my life.* Jesus is speaking into that and saying that you're mistaken.

In a piece written by *Village Voice* columnist Cynthia Heimel, she argues that modern people often think that if only we could make it in our chosen business, then we would be happy. She has seen so many people in New York City who are trying to be aspiring actors—but, of course, you don't just show up to the city and then make it to Broadway. You have to do a lot of different things, and get a few breaks here and there. To get by as they live in New York City, these aspiring actors will have to take on other types of work in order to get by. They are extremely stressed and anxious. Heimel would see some of these individuals actually make a name for themselves and eventually make it on Broadway. She says that at that point, they are no longer nervous, anxious, insecure, or stressed; rather, they are now insufferable—and, of course, that's corrosive to their relationships. (In fact, soon enough their very success makes them anxious, insecure, or stressed, since now they must maintain that position, so they're now looking over their shoulder the whole time.) Heimel is suggesting that we tend to think that if only we could achieve our goals, so that we had no more "if onlys," then our lives would be good and we'd be happy. What Heimel is saying is that if only you get what you're striving for, guess what? You're not actually going to be happy. You're going to be more unhappy (*If You Can't Live Without Me, Why Aren't You Dead Yet?!*, pages 13-14).

> God says there is something deeper and greater than our "if onlys."

God is concerned about something deeper. And he's not only sympathetic; he's actually done something about it. He can now enter into a person's life and deal with the main problem. God says that there is something deeper and greater that needs to be addressed than all those "if onlys" in our lives; and that, when he deals with our ultimate problem, we'll have perspective on those "if onlys," whether we continue to live with them, or whether we move beyond them. That is why he says of his coming ruler, in Micah **5:5**, that "he shall be their peace." That's not just peace from war, but a holistic peace—a form of human flourishing: shalom. Not only peace from war, but even from the warfare that is raging in people's hearts because of sin.

Questions for reflection

1. What makes you ask yourself, *Does God care?* How might these verses help you shape an answer?

2. How *would* you complete the sentence, *If only God would come and give _____ to me*?

3. What changed perspective would you have on your "if onlys," and what peace might you experience, if you knew that God had already dealt with your ultimate problem?

PART TWO

The Restorer Is Unexpected

5:2 is perhaps the most famous verse of the entire book, read each Christmas in churches around the world: "But you, O Bethlehem Ephrathah, who are too little to be among the clans of Judah, from you shall come forth for me one who is to be ruler in Israel, whose coming forth is from of old, from ancient days." This is a messianic prophecy that would be fulfilled in the person of Jesus, as Matthew makes clear (Matthew 2:1-6). Micah **5:3** gives us hints of the context and the setting in which Jesus would enter. All of this amounts to the fact that there is unexpectedness in this majesty. This restorer, this messianic figure who would bring peace into our lives, would be born in Bethlehem Ephrathah. Bethlehem was such a small town that it wasn't even listed by Joshua when he was looking at all the 150 towns and cities that were in the area (see David Prior, *Joel, Micah, Habakkuk*, page 158). That's how insignificant it was. It was notable only for being the town that King David's family was from (1 Samuel 16:1-5)—and for nothing else.

And so this is the unexpectedness of this restorer. He would come from a very small town, which seems very weak. God often does things upside down, subversively. The passage emphasizes the weakness of this restorer—but then in the same verse, we discover that he is also strong. Weakness and strength, humility and power, do not usually co-exist. But here we find an unexpected restorer who comes in a gentle and weak way, but who, at the same time, is "from of old."

The word here for "old" is used only two other times in the Old Testament—once in Habakkuk 1 and once in Deuteronomy 33. In both instances, the word is used as an adjective to describe God. In Habakkuk 1:12 it says, "Are you not from everlasting [or "of old"], O LORD my God, my Holy One?" In Deuteronomy 33:27 we read, "The eternal [or "of old"] God is your dwelling place." Here in Micah it's describing the restorer who would come in the future. Here, it's describing a baby, born of a woman through the normal way—through pregnancy, labor, and delivery (Micah **5:3**).

Jesus' mother Mary had a child who was older than she was. His origins were of old, from ancient days. Mary and her husband Joseph had authority as his parents but he had authority as their eternal God. We see this in his naming. To name something is to manage it. This is the reason why parents have been given the privilege of naming their children. Your name was probably given you by your parent(s) or guardian. There is power in naming; and who named Jesus?

"The angel said to [Mary], 'Do not be afraid, Mary, for you have found favor with God. And behold, you will conceive in your womb and bear a son, and you shall call his name Jesus.'"

(Luke 1:30-31)

"An angel of the Lord appeared to [Mary's fiancé Joseph] in a dream, saying, 'Joseph, son of David, do not fear to take Mary as your wife, for that which is conceived in her is from the Holy Spirit. She will bear a son, and you shall call his name Jesus, for he will save his people from their sins.'" (Matthew 1:20-21)

An angel came and announced what the name of the child was going to be. Jesus came humbly, but he was also unmanageable. He came from Bethlehem, "too little to be among the clans of Judah" (Micah **5:2**), but he also came from heaven, too great to be described. He is of old. He comes born in a manger, weak and humble, but at the same time,

> He was born in a manger, but no one can manage him. He is unnameable, untameable.

no one can manage him. He is unnameable, untameable. That's who this ruler is. No human being can manage Jesus. Jesus manages you. He names you; we don't name him.

Oftentimes when we think about Jesus, we think of him as something like a domesticated cat to which we can say "Come here." But we repeatedly find this king being referred to as a lion. It's paradoxical. He is the Lion of Judah, but he is also the Lamb of God. He is a lion-hearted Lamb, but a Lamb-like lion.

This is what's so beautiful about our restorer. If he is only humble, weak and near to us, then he can empathize with our feelings, but he can't do anything to change or deliver us from our circumstances. If he only has power and is of old, if he is magnificent and majestic, if he is the Lion of Judah, then he has the power to change our lives, but he seems uncaring and detached from us. But what this passage is showing is that our restorer is both good and great.

"Jesus" has this way of identifying with the ordinary, but at the same time, he isn't merely ordinary. He was ordinary in the sense that he had a name like "Jesus," which was a common name; he was also born in a manger, had a common trade, and grew up in an obscure village. But on the other hand, he was the Savior, God, the Lord. He was Yahweh himself. The restorer was unexpected, and that's the kind of restorer we need.

The Restorer Is Strong and Majestic

What will this humble, powerful restorer do?

"He shall stand and shepherd his flock in the strength of the LORD,
in the majesty of the name of the LORD his God. And they shall
dwell secure, for now he shall be great to the ends of the earth.
And he shall be their peace." (Micah **5:4-5a**)

The category God chooses to use to describe his coming ruler is "shepherd"—he is a shepherd who will rule in the name and majesty of God. He is a gentle shepherd who is going to provide for the needs of the flock, but at the same time he comes in the name and majesty of the great God. Here is a divine shepherd—and we, at this point in salvation history, know his human name was, and is, Jesus.

Micah 5 is the context that helps us appreciate Jesus' famous words in John 10:14: "I am the good shepherd. I know my own and my own know me." He is the great shepherd. When the shepherd of the flock comes, he rules his flock with gentleness, being aware of their needs. In the end, what God is asking and requiring of his people is not perfection, but submission; he does not call us to be flawless, but to follow.

As Tim Keller pointed out in a sermon on John 10 (entitled "The Good Shepherd," July 14, 1991), deep within our hearts we all long for a shepherd to come and care for our needs. If and when we have problems, we want to know if there is anyone out there who is able to take care of us. Is there someone out there who is going to make everything right? Is there someone who is going to bring control in the midst of all my chaos?

We are looking for a shepherd. But where do we find one? If you are single, and if you have thoughts of being married, then you might think that perhaps your future spouse could be that individual. For those of you who are married, perhaps that's what you were thinking before you were married. But then what happened?! Surprise! Your husband or wife is not even close to being the shepherd that you thought he or she would be.

Some of us think that our parents are the ones who are going to take care of our needs. Others look to our nation's leader, or the person we wish to be our nation's leader. We all want somebody to be our shepherd, and to rule us, and bring us to the place where we think we need to be. We get surprised and disappointed, even angry, when we discover that none of those people can truly meet our expectations.

Given that others must disappoint us, many of us look closer to home for a shepherd: to ourselves. But ultimately, if you live with the weight of trying to shepherd your own life, that's a lot of responsibility. You might be very self-sufficient. You might be very gifted and possess all sorts of abilities, competencies, aspirations, and potential. But if you believe that you can be the ultimate shepherd of your life, that exerts great pressure. Why? Because if we're honest with ourselves, we know that we're not qualified for that position. We are under-qualified, or possibly disqualified; we are not competent to do that kind of work. That's why we wrestle with this over and over again. What we ultimately need is somebody who will come and shepherd us in a gentle yet powerful way.

Jesus is the eternal, all-powerful, unexpected, humble, Good Shepherd. He is the leader and guide that all of us seek for. He seeks his sheep, he guides us into fresh pasture, and he protects us; ultimately, he laid down his life for us. He is our divine Shepherd. And he is supremely, uniquely, perfectly good at it.

Deuteronomy 33:12 says:

"Let the beloved of the LORD rest secure in him,
> for he shields him all day long,
> and the one the LORD loves rests between his shoulders."

(NIV)

What an amazing image! The one who is beloved, the one who follows the LORD as his sheep, dwells in safety because he dwells between God's shoulders.

So picture this. God's children are resting between God's shoulders. As Keller put it in his sermon on John 10, we're walking along with God on his journey; we're his children and he cares for us; and he says, *Getting tired? Straying off? Get on my shoulders.* The beloved rest and dwell between the shoulders of God. God is saying that he wants us to rest on his shoulders. He wants us to know that he's not only sympathetic and knows our needs, but he is somebody who can actually do something about them.

> God's children are resting between God's shoulders.

He is an unexpected restorer who comes in gentleness, but also with power and ability. He is the Shepherd who is going to rule you, the beloved, in such a way that you'll be able to dwell in safety and security because he will be your peace.

Are you lost? Are you toiling? Are you restless? Are you wondering whether or not God is going to help and deliver you? He promises he will. And, as we look at the cross, we know that he already has. He may lead us through a period of trials, exile, or difficult circumstances, but that's not because God doesn't care. He has an ear to the ground; he's sympathetic. He knows your real needs. He knows your needs better than you know your own needs. Our main problem is not just our suffering; it is our sin. God rescues us from our sin and restores us for the life we long for. He does it by himself coming to be our Shepherd, who cares for his flock. If you're on his back, he will carry you. He will be our peace.

Questions for reflection

1. How does this section make you more excited as you look ahead to next Christmas?!

2. Do you tend to over-focus on Jesus as humble and weak, or as powerful and strong? What difference does this make to your life when you sin… when things go wrong… when you need help?

3. "If you're on his back, he will carry you." How is that going to transform your day? Do you need to share this great truth with a struggling brother or sister?

7. SELF-SUFFICIENT OR GOD-DEPENDENT?

Self-sufficiency and self-reliance are the order of our day. It's why we don't like hearing that we need to be rescued.

There is a huge market today for do-it-yourself manuals and self-help titles. For instance, in the Self-Sufficiency series, there's one book entitled, *The Ultimate Self-Sufficiency Handbook: A Complete Guide to Baking, Crafts, Gardening, Preserving your Harvest, Raising Animals, and More.* These self-help, Self-Sufficiency manuals are **oxymoronic**—if you're sufficient enough to be able to figure things out, then why do you need a manual to assist you?

Most of us wouldn't be so crass as to announce, "I'm self-sufficient." Many of us are not that obvious; we're a little more sophisticated in disguising our aspirations to self-sufficiency. It comes out in a more indirect way where the common sentiment might be something like, "I want to have enough money that I don't have to think about money." Or put another way, "I want to be in control, comfortable, and able to take advantage of all the resources and benefits at my disposal even though I have certain outside forces bearing down on me that could cause me to cave in."

In this context, dependency is not acceptable in our life view. We think dependency is for those who are weak. It's for hard cases and lost causes, but not those like us who have life figured out, who are doing well at life, and who therefore highly value independence. Many of us like self-made people. We like successful entrepreneurs.

We like pioneers. We like trailblazers. We like people who are inno-vative and creative. So the idea of rescue is unpalatable. It's not well received. "I don't need rescue; I just need a different angle, a different approach, and different perspective. Most of the time I am able to fend for myself."

In the book of Micah, God is dealing with a people who are in desperate need of being rescued. They need to know that they need it. And so do we. There are three needs for rescue in this passage. First, the need to be rescued from our obstacles. Second, the need to be rescued from self. Third, the need to be rescued from the outside.

Rescue from Obstacles

Micah simultaneously forecasts the invasion and the rescue of God's people. How can that happen? He talks about invasion, and at the same time, he talks about how they'll be rescued. The Assyrian army will eventually fall upon Israel. They will get so close that they will be treading upon their palaces. King Sennacherib would get so close that, as noted in the last chapter, he would be able to offend and hu-miliate the king of Israel, Hezekiah (5:1). Sennacherib would be able to insult him and slap him on his cheek. And there's nothing Hezekiah could do to respond to him.

But there will be an uprising during which the Assyrians will be caught off guard by the strength of what God will provide for the Israelites. "We will raise against [the Assyrian] seven shepherds and eight princes of men; they shall shepherd the land of Assyria with the sword, and the land of Nimrod at its entrances; and he shall de-liver us from the Assyrian when he comes into our land and treads within our border" (**v 5b-6**). The "seven shepherds and eight princ-es" is a figurative phrase, indicating that there will be many leaders whom God will raise up for his purposes. They make up a team of "under-shepherds" that are led by and carry out the will of the great shepherd of verse 4 (just as elders are called to do in the New Testa-ment church—see 1 Peter 5:1-4).

Next, God makes a promise in Micah **5:7**, that "the remnant of Jacob shall be in the midst of many peoples like dew from the LORD, like showers on the grass." The word "remnant" is not the special, good people among the inhabitants of Israel and Judah. No, the word is simply used to refer to God's people—sinners whom God has saved. Further (and crucially), the remnant is not some separate group who need to keep themselves withdrawn from everyone else: "The remnant of Jacob shall be ... in the midst of many peoples." God's people are going to live among them.

> God's people are called to be a blessing and a benefit.

God further describes his remnant with an image of dew or showers. In the Bible, especially in the Old Testament, references to rivers, streams, rain, showers, and dew are usually agricultural or irrigation metaphors referring to the blessings of God. The Middle East was an arid place, so having any form of water was a blessing. God's people are called to be a blessing and a benefit to those who are around them—their neighbors, their society, and their community.

But there will also be victory for God's people: "The remnant of Jacob shall be among the nations, in the midst of many peoples, like a lion among the beasts of the forest, like a young lion among the flocks of sheep, which, when it goes through, treads down and tears in pieces, and there is none to deliver. Your hand shall be lifted up over your adversaries, and all your enemies shall be cut off" (**v 8-9**). The Assyrian will have a day of treading over God's people. But there will be a time in the future, in a period when the Messiah will come (v 2), when the remnant, the people of God, will do the treading. The treading refers to the inevitable progress of the people of God in the Messianic era, when they will not depend on the weapons of war (4:3) but rather on the triumphant victory of the Messiah over sin (see Colossians 2:15). This is an already-but-not-yet type of triumph, where the already-come ultimate triumph of God through Christ on the cross takes hold of us and shapes us to see how we ought to live in this world—a world that is still far from experiencing fullness of the new heavens and the new earth. So at the same time as being called to "tread," the people of God have been called to be a blessing to those around them and a representative of the God who loves them; to rule and to shepherd just like our Messiah, who is the shepherd.

National to Individual

Again, the Gospels show us how what Micah promises on a national level to Israel works on an individual level too. In Jesus' day, we find a "remnant" of those who are truly God's people, among the inhabitants of Israel. There's a great narrative in Mark 5:21-43, in which Jesus arrives in a town and meets a couple of people. The first person is a Jewish ruler, a synagogue member, whose name is Jairus. Then Jesus meets a woman who has been subject to bleeding for 12 years. She is unnamed. This is the way it happened in ancient culture—when you were somebody who was very important, you had a name. But if you were someone who was marginalized, you were referred to as the woman, or the man, or the person with the disability. That's why, when the Bible actually names the blind man Bartimaeus (Mark 10:46), that's very uncommon.

Jairus is the first of the two to meet Jesus. He comes and bows down to him and says, *I know that you have the ability and power to perform miracles, and I need your help. My little daughter is dying. Could you please come and help?* What does Jesus do? He goes along with his disciples to Jairus' home and there's a crowd following them. While they're on their way to Jairus' home, this woman who has been subject to bleeding for 12 years—this unnamed woman—thinks to herself, *If I could just touch the hem of his garment, then I'll be healed. I'm not going to bother him. No one will know. This is what I'll do.* She does this in the middle of their journey over to Jairus' home and what happens? Jesus stops. He says, "Who touched my garments?" (Mark 5:30). The disciples say, *What are you talking about? Everyone's touching you; everyone's around you. Let's move on. We've got an im-portant thing to do here.* Jesus says, *No, I felt power leaving me, and somebody touched me.* Imagine what's going on in the mind of Jairus right now. If you're the father and your daughter is dying, and Jesus stops just to have an unnecessary conversation with a woman whom he's already helped, you would probably be anxious to the point of going crazy. Jairus is probably thinking, *We don't have time for this, Jesus. What kind of a prophet and healer are you?*

Tim Keller puts it this way: If two people come into the hospital emergency room and one has a chronic but non-emergency condi-tion, like this woman, and then in comes a little girl who is about to die, the medics need to have the wisdom and sense to prioritize. They address the potentially fatal condition first. The other person might be in pain, but she's not going to die from her condition, so she has to wait. You deal with the person who's about to die, and then you take care of the other. But Jesus doesn't work this way. He's a lot more complicated than you think. He's certainly not predictable, or manage-able (see *King's Cross,* page 62).

Then it gets worse for Jairus. He hears the news that he most doesn't want to hear. Men from his home come and tell him that his daughter has died. There's no need to trouble the teacher any-more. What do you think—besides the fact that Jairus would have been devastated by that news—was going on in his mind? *Jesus, that's why I was telling you we needed to hurry! What were you doing stopping for this woman? She could've waited! What were you thinking?!*

Most of us can empathize in the sense that we have found our-selves in circumstances where we're not sure exactly why things are happening the way they're happening. We can't come up with an explanation. We look at God and we say, "Can't you do better than this?" That's where Jairus is.

Jesus then looks at Jairus and says, "Do not fear, only believe" (Mark 5:36). He's telling Jairus, *I know the circumstances. They don't look great right now, but trust me, because it's not like how it seems right now.* In the moment we might not have the correct vision and perspective, just as Jairus doesn't have the correct perspective. He's overwhelmed by the present circumstances. Jesus, who is **omniscient** and has the ultimate perspective is able to look into the future, and he says, "Do not fear, only believe."

> Jesus is able to look into the future, and he says, "Do not fear."

They arrive at Jairus' home and there's a commotion, obviously. People are wailing and crying, and Jesus says:

"'Why are you making a commotion and weeping? The child is not dead but sleeping.' And they laughed at him. But he put them all outside and took the child's father and mother and those who were with him and went in where the child was. Taking her by the hand he said to her, 'Talitha cumi,' which means, 'Little girl, I say to you, arise.' And immediately the girl got up and began walking (for she was twelve years of age), and they were immediately overcome with amazement."

(Mark 5:39-42)

Jairus came to Jesus asking him to heal his daughter from her illness. And Jesus shows them the resurrection.

Keller writes:

"Be aware that when you go to Jesus for help, you will give to him and you will get from him more than you bargained for in most instances." (*King's Cross*, page 64)

Take Jairus. Presumably, he thought, *I'm going to bring Jesus to heal my daughter, and we'll just be able to move on with our lives.* Or the woman, who thought, *I'm just going to touch his cloak and quietly disappear. I'm not supposed to be out in public because I'll be declared unclean by the priest. But that's OK, because no one will know*

I'm here and I'll be gone. They both end up receiving more and giving more than they had initially planned.

Oftentimes we go to God for help. We have all sorts of external obstacles in our lives and we want God to help us. But that's all we want from him. There are a few moments when we realize that we're not as self-sufficient as we thought we were, so we want God's help during those moments. But Jairus ended up getting more than he expected and giving more than he bargained for. Why? Because Jesus didn't just say, *Here's my help. You're welcome. Have a nice life.* No. He looked at Jairus and said, *Trust me. You're going to need to give over control to me. You're going to need to give up your agenda. You're going to need to believe in me instead of giving way to fear. And as you do that, I'm going to give you more than you thought possible.*

What about the sick woman? Jesus stops and asks who touched him. He causes her to publicly acknowledge what she's done and what she needs. She has to humble herself: *Yes, I'm the person who touched you.* Then he doesn't just move her on after healing her—he says, "Daughter, your faith has made you well" (Mark 5:34). She ends up getting far more than she bargained for. Jesus has realigned her entire universe. She gives more than just, *I'm just going to touch him and then leave.* In the end, she has to publicly come forward and confess what has happened and what she believes about him.

This is what the Israelites would experience, Micah said. They would want God to get rid of the Assyrians, to help them to overcome their enemy. But what would God do? He would give them more than they bargained for. He would raise up a shepherd, and under-shepherds, who would deliver the people (Micah **5:5b-6**). And that's all Israel really wanted. *Great, God, thanks so much. Now we can be left alone and enjoy peace.* But God doesn't stop there. He tells them that they are going to be a blessing to all nations and be his representatives and rule and shepherd. They're not going to live in isolation as the remnant. Instead they will be among all these people. He's going to reassign and realign everything that they thought they needed to do. When God gets involved with us in order to rescue us, he asks us to give far more to him than we had expected, and we find ourselves receiving far more from him than we had ever thought to ask for.

Questions for reflection

1. Think about the people you look up to. What does that tell you about which characteristics you prize in someone?

2. Do you ever go to God for help with a situation, but want him to leave your deeper problems (and idols) alone?

3. How have you experienced God asking for far more of you than you'd expected, but at the same time giving you far more than you'd asked for?

PART TWO

Rescue From Obstacles

Israel would have been content had God's promise ended with the assurance that the Assyrians would be defeated. But even once God had promised them far more than they would ask for in **verses 7-9**, God was still not done with his rescue. There was a weightier call that they needed to acknowledge—that is, the rescue from themselves.

Why do we need to be rescued from ourselves? Even if we don't mind being helped with problems outside of ourselves, we don't like to hear that we need to be rescued from ourselves. Our ultimate fear is to be dependent. We don't want to be sick because we don't want others to help us. We want to care for ourselves. We fear bankruptcy because it'll expose that we're not competent or rich. We fear academic failure because perhaps people might think that we're not smart enough. We fear losing our jobs because maybe people will think that we're not good enough. We want to succeed, and we want to succeed in our own strength.

> Israel had developed all kinds of strategies to avoid the indignity of needing to be rescued.

Israel had developed all kinds of strategies to avoid the indignity of needing to be rescued. Horses, chariots, cities, and strongholds were all aimed at gaining strength and providing refuge (**v 10-11**); sorceries and fortune-tellers predicted and promised to affect the future (**v 12**); their idols would give them fulfillment (**v 13**). What is God's response to their self-help strategies? He takes them away. He cuts these things off. It looks as though God is denying instead of giving; as though he's not blessing, but rather is taking away and cursing; that he does not want to be generous and gracious, but rather to deprive them. It seems that way on the surface. But that's not what's going on at all. He's denying them or taking away from them these things because of his love for them. He's trying to protect them from pursuing their own self-help strategies, which will only lead to a dead-end. There are four things he's going to do:

1. He plans to take away their military power and their ability to fight for themselves. "I will cut off your horses from among you and will destroy your chariots" (**v 10**). So ask yourself: What do you look to for your power? Where do you find your strength?

2. He plans to cut off their places of retreat and refuge. "I will cut off the cities of your land and throw down all your strongholds" (**v 11**). Cities represented safety. What do you look to for protection and security?

3. He plans to cut off their attempt to control the future. "I will cut off sorceries from your hand, and you shall have no more tellers of fortunes" (**v 12**). How do you attempt to control your future? What do you worry about in your future? Which decisions cause you stress because you feel that on their outcome hangs your future happiness?

4. He plans to cut off all of their idols—to separate them from allegiances to false gods, and to help and rescue them. "I will cut off your carved images and your pillars from among you, and you shall bow down no more to the work of your hands; and I will root out your Asherah images from among you and destroy your cities" (**v 13-14**). These things refer to the pagan foreign gods, Baal and Asherah. When worshiping them, the people would engage in **cultic** sexual prostitution. **Verse 15** is another reminder of how seriously God takes spiritual unfaithfulness to him.

We might say, "I'm not involved in that sort of thing, so I can be excused. I'm not like the Israelites engaged in that kind of activity. I'm good. I'm not engaged in idolatry like the Israelites were." But the message that Baal and Asherah gave to the Israelites was that they could control their fertility and be blessed in that area. That comes close to home for many of us. Don't we pursue the things that we trust will be able to guarantee in our lives (now and in the future) fruitfulness, productivity, effectiveness, and financial gain?

These were the four self-help strategies that the Israelites had, and God's approach in dealing with them was "I will cut off... I will cut off... I will cut off... I will cut off..." (**v 10-13**). His rescue involved taking them away. He was promising to rescue the Israelites from themselves.

I Happened

There's a very insightful passage in Thomas Harris's novel *The Silence of the Lambs*. The monstrous individual Hannibal Lecter is in a conversation with Officer Starling. He's describing all the terrible and evil things he's done in his life. She's obviously overwhelmed and she asks him some questions: "What happened to you that you could do this? Who did something to you that you could be so bad?" She wants an explanation. *How could you end up this way?* His response is, "Nothing happened to me. I happened." His point is, *You can't reduce me to, or explain me with, a set of external influences.*

It's so easy for us to think about being rescued from all of the terrible things that are out there, or indeed from people and circumstances that are merely annoying. But we don't tend to think that we need to be rescued from ourselves. Yet the truth is that humanity doesn't simply need assistance; we need rescue. We don't need support; we need salvation. We don't merely need help; we need wholesale redemption. Even if all our external circumstances were positive and peaceful, we would still be sinners. We would still be idolaters. "There is nothing outside a person that by going into him can defile him, but the things that come out of a person are what defile him," says Jesus (Mark 7:15). It's why God's work of conversion and renewal is not skin-deep, but at the level of our hearts (Romans 2:28-29).

Again, we see this on a personal level in the Gospels. Consider the two people Jesus interacts with in John 3 and 4. First, there is a religious leader: Nicodemus. He's a religious insider and a moral conformist. Next, there is a Samaritan woman who is a social outcast and has had five husbands, and now lives with a man to whom she is not married. Jesus interacts with them differently. He gives them different things because they have different struggles and needs—although the bottom line is that they're both striving to be their own rescuer. The woman doesn't have meaning or acceptance. That's why she's in and out of relationships. She goes to a well in the heat of the day, on her own, showing her social exclusion because, presumably, she wants to go at a time when the other women of her community are not around to ridicule her. But there she meets this man who says, *I will give you something that you need. You don't even realize what you need, but I'm going to give you living water.* She has this insatiable desire to find meaning, acceptance, and probably dignity... but she hasn't found it. She has kept on going after relationships, thinking this man or that man would prove to be her savior—someone in whom she'd find meaning and acceptance and dignity. And then Jesus comes and provides her with living water. He knows everything about her, and he loves and welcomes her anyway.

> *You don't need a lecture; you need to be born again, Jesus says.*

Nicodemus is very different. Here is a religious person who thinks he is all good. He is not a moral outcast who ought to be shunned. He is someone who is respected in the community. He is a **Pharisee**: a learned person. He is respectable. How does Jesus respond to him? He goes directly at him and says, *You need to be born again.* He is not as gentle as he was with the woman; Nicodemus has come wanting to have a theological conversation. But Jesus is not interested in lecturing him. *You don't need a lecture; you need to be born again,* he says.

Religious or totally irreligious, we all have our own self-help strategies and make our own attempts at self-sufficiency—but they won't get it done. We need a Savior, a Rescuer. We need the Lord himself. We need him to rescue us by cutting off from us those things we love too much and look to for rescue. We need him to show us that he is always enough.

Rescued From Outside

Ultimately, we don't rescue ourselves from external circumstances and opposition, nor from ourselves; we're rescued from outside of ourselves. The One who would rescue Israel was not Israel: "He shall deliver us from the Assyrian when he comes into our land and treads within our border" (Micah **5:6**). This is referring to the messianic figure mentioned in verses 4-5a: "And he shall stand and shepherd his flock in the strength of the LORD, in the majesty of the name of the LORD his God … he shall be great to the ends of the earth. And he shall be their peace." This "he," the deliverer and rescuer, the redeemer, is Jesus— verse 2 is quoted in Matthew 2:6, showing that Jesus is the fulfillment of this prophecy about the "king of the Jews" (Matthew 2:1).

God is saying, *I want to rescue you, not reject you. I want to deliver you, not destroy you.* How can a holy God rescue an idolatrous people who deserve rejection because, to use Hannibal Lecter's insight, *they* happened? Because Jesus received the rejection that we deserved, he achieved the rescue that we desperately need. He is our Rescuer. Israel needed to learn that; so must we.

If you go after any other savior, you're only going to be disappointed, for if you meet its demands, it will not fulfill you. And if you fail to meet its standards, it will not forgive you. If your career fails, it will never forgive you. Jesus is the only Savior who, if you gain him, will satisfy you; but who, if you fail him, will forgive you. No other savior will do that. No other system will do that. Jesus will. His rescue is greater than we would ever think to ask for, it is deeper than we would ever think we needed, and it gives us a relationship with him that provides a satisfaction that will never run out throughout our eternity.

Questions for reflection

1. "Our ultimate fear is to be dependent." Is this true of you? What would your prayer life suggest is the answer to that question? If you do fear dependence, how does this affect your relationship with God?

2. What "self-help strategies" might God need to "cut off" from you? Will you actually ask him to show you an accurate answer, and then to do the cutting work?

3. How is Jesus a better Savior than the things that rival him in your life or society? How will this motivate you to worship and live for him alone?

8. WHAT DOES THE LORD REQUIRE OF YOU?

We began our journey through Micah by saying that oftentimes it's the difficult things in life and the hard words that we need more than the easy days and the soothing words. When you're sick, the last thing you need is someone to tell you that things are okay. You need someone to tell you that you are sick, and how you can get better. We always need to keep in mind that this is what Micah is doing. And in chapter 6, the topic is justice. Hear this as a gentle physician telling you, "Unless you heed these words, the infection may get worse."

The Importance of Justice

Here's how our scene starts: God summons his creation (**v 1-2**). God is looking for a tribunal before whom he can bring formal, legal charges—his "indictment"—against his people. Notice that we don't actually get to hear the content of his charges, but there is a reason for that. In ancient times, writings like these functioned a lot more like letters than they did like books. Typically, they'd be read in public settings from start to finish without a break. The reason that Micah doesn't bring the charges here is because he has already done so earlier in the book:

- In Micah 2, the charge was that God's people have zero regard in their hearts for the weak and poor (2:1-2).

- In Micah 3, the indictment was the fact that they all (from greatest to least) have power in some way, shape, or form—yet they use power not for the good for everyone, but just for themselves and those close to them (3:1-3).

- In Micah 1, we saw how all of this is driven at bottom by their desires. They become so malformed, so curled inward, that a life that's lived this way (one that is just about me, mine, and my stuff) has actually come to seem normal to them. God's message through his prophet Micah is that everything we see here is not okay. There is a serious problem.

But... these are God's people, in God's land, conducting their worship in his temple according to his laws. Isn't that the main thing? Surely that counts for something?

After all, for an ancient Jew, the single most important thing in life was worship: to "come before the LORD" (**6:6**) at the temple with something in hand to offer and sacrifice to him. But Micah—and don't miss how controversial this would have been—utterly debunks this central notion. "Will the LORD be pleased" with overflowing sacrificial offerings (**v 7**)? No—because doing "what is good" (**v 8**) is about more (though not less) than showing up to worship God at the temple. The basic point here is that God is not pleased if we elevate one aspect of what he requires of us as his people, while ignoring the rest. The whole enterprise is a sham if it doesn't come from a life lived in pursuit of justice.

Micah says that you can bring burnt offerings (**v 6**)—for a Jew at this time, these would have been the most costly, because all the other offerings allowed a portion to be taken home to eat, but the whole of a burnt offering was given to the fire. Micah says you can offer the things that are the best (**v 7**), the cream of the crop: calves a year old, thousands of rams, rivers of oil, your firstborn child... all of this was meant to sound absurd. Micah says, in the language of today, that you can give everything that means anything: your time, your money, your possessions, your goods, doing church until you're blue in the face—but it's all a sham if it doesn't crystallize as concrete love for your neighbors. That's the point here.

The LORD said something similar through his prophet Amos:

"I hate, I despise your feasts, and I take no delight in your solemn assemblies. Even though you offer me your burnt offerings and grain offerings, I will not accept them; and the peace offerings of your fattened animals, I will not look upon them. Take away from me the noise of your songs; to the melody of your harps I will not listen. But let justice roll down like waters, and righteousness like an ever-flowing stream." (Amos 5:21-24)

Jesus had the same issue with religious practice that was not accompanied by pursuing justice because it was not flowing out of a loving heart. The Pharisees—who were very devoted, Scripture-soaked members of God's people, and therefore, in some ways, the evangelical Christians of their day—found themselves being lashed by his tongue: "Woe to you, scribes and Pharisees, hypocrites! For you **tithe** mint and dill and cumin, and have neglected the weightier matters of the law: justice and mercy and faithfulness. These you ought to have done, without neglecting the others" (Matthew 23:23).

Nicholas Wolterstorff, an emeritus professor at Yale, is well worth quoting at length here:

"The witness of the prophets is that worship loses its authenticity when those who participate in it do not practice and struggle for justice. Let us allow ourselves to be surprised, astonished, taken aback by this. In worship we sing hymns of praise to God. Why isn't it enough that we do this with awareness and intensity? In worship we ask God to give bread to those who lack it. Can't we mean that when the words are said? If we mean it, isn't it enough? The reason we feel this way is because we've understood worship either as a device for **curetting** favor with God or as an occasion to escape from ordinary life. On these understandings, the suggestion that injustice would bleed worship of its authenticity is just nonsensical. The critique of the prophets is grounded in the conviction that the whole point of worship is to give expression to the commitment of our lives to God. The point of worship is not the performance of certain self-contained actions, no matter how sincere and appropriate those actions. Worship is for giving voice to life, to lives of faith oriented to God. Justice is an integral component to such a life. This is why worship in the absence of justice does not please God. Why, it nauseates him. It's so seriously malformed that God finds it disgusting. But let me emphasize that the prophets are not saying merely that God wants justice as well as prayer, mercy as well as praise, love as well as worship. It is not both worship and justice, but rather not authentic worship unless justice." (*Hearing the Call*, page 43)

What Is Justice?

So we need to get a handle on the nature of what justice is. Micah **6:8** defines it: "He has told you, O man, what is good; and what does the LORD require of you but to do justice, and to love kindness, and to walk humbly with your God?"

Two phrases here reveal the true nature of justice: "do justice" and "love kindness."

When we think of doing justice, we typically think of something like performing retribution. Most people equate justice with punishing wrongs. That's certainly part of what justice entails, but it's actually much broader than that. It is certainly giving the perpetrators their due, but doing justice is also giving those who cannot stand up for themselves—the victims, the poor, the powerless, the vulnerable, the voiceless—their due as well. It is more than only punishing wrong; it is creating a situation and a society where everything is right—a society where every last person in it, including the most vulnerable and the weakest, can flourish and thrive. That's what doing justice, according to the Bible, really means.

In ancient Jewish culture, the word Micah uses for "kindness" (*hesed*) could also be translated as unqualified love; limitless love;

stubborn, unceasing, dogged love that says, "I refuse to give up on you, even if everyone else tells me that I should." It is a loving kindness that says, "I will not budge in my loyalty to you. I will stay with you even in the moments when there's nothing in it for me." That's what kindness was understood to be.

When we couple these two phrases, we get a clearer sense of what the nature of justice is. It's loving so deeply, so fully and stubbornly, that we refuse to budge until everyone, including the most vulnerable of society, can flourish and thrive. That is the nature of justice. It puts many modern conceptions of justice to shame. It likely puts many of us to shame too.

In his work *Our Kids*, the American political scientist Robert Putnam points out that there used to be a sense that every single kid in our town was "our kid." All of our neighbors were ours and we were responsible for one another, so that when one person fell, it was our job to stoop down and pick them up. We don't have that commitment anymore. Putnam argues that this loss of social cohesion is one of the primary causes of social injustice today.

Injustice and inequality grow where *hesed* shrivels. We are better at making excuses for injustice in our societies than we are at committing to each other and asking what *hesed* would do for another. And this is precisely Micah's message.

Remember...

How do we know God cares about justice? Because God has exercised justice, and his people know that. Why does God insist that his people show *hesed*? Because God has displayed such overflowing *hesed*, and his people know that. He "brought you up from the land of Egypt and redeemed you from the house of slavery … O my people, remember…" (**v 4-5**).

Micah is recalling the bedrock event in Israel's history. For centuries, God's people had lived under the oppressive yoke of the Egyptian regime. But God—in his kindness, in his *hesed*—raised up leaders like Moses, Aaron, and Miriam to free them from oppression. As they were going to the land God had promised to give them, traveling from Shittim to Gilgal (**v 5**), God's people were assaulted again, in particular by a king of Moab named Balak (Numbers 22). God raised up a prophet, Balaam, and a talking donkey to thwart the Moabite forces and to protect his people (Numbers 22 – 24). "Remember…" says God. But by Micah's time, despite everything God had done, his people were effectively telling him, *Man, we wish you weren't around here anymore. Look, we go to the temple, and do the offerings. What more do you want? Why be so demanding?*

This is why God asks, "O my people, what have I done to you? How have I wearied you? Answer me!" (Micah **6:3**). The answer, of course, is that God hasn't done anything to weary them. They are the ones who have wearied him. Then effectively, in **verses 4-5**, he looks them in the eye, grabs them by the collar, and says, *I will never leave you, I will never forsake you. I will show to you a love that is far more resilient, far more stubborn even than you are. I will melt and unlock your vaulted hearts with a hesed that burns more brightly and hotly than any love you've ever known.* Micah is trying to grab the hearts of his people as he relays the words of God: *Do you remember that love that means that I looked on you and cared for you and redeemed you and blessed you, not because you deserved it, but because I loved you (compare Deuteronomy 7:7-8)? Remember that love.*

> God looks them in the eye and says, *I will show you a love that is more stubborn even than you are.*

Had Micah been around today, he would have pointed us back to a different bedrock event in the history of God's people. He didn't have the privilege of seeing it, but we do, and we need to remember it. God came again in his stubborn love for his people, showing and calling for justice and loving kindness—and once more his people grew weary of him. They said, *Man, we just wish you weren't around anymore.* They saw justice and *hesed* walking humbly among them and it made them mad because they saw how far they had fallen from what God wanted from his people. So they perpetrated the most unjust and least loving act of all time—they killed God's Son. And yet at the same moment, God's *hesed* was unceasing and dogged, and so he purposed that that same bitterly unjust death would be the means of justice, as his Son's death was counted in our place; it would be the means of overflowing love, as his Son's life was reckoned as ours. This is the gospel in one word: *hesed.*

And so it is God's *hesed* that empowers ours. It is God's justice that motivates ours. It is remembering who God is that reshapes who we are. If we walk humbly with our God, we will love to be like our God. So, we must open the vault of our hearts. One of the primary ways we can enact this loving kindness and justice is directly with those around us. If we can begin to steer our gaze away from ourselves and onto others, especially those on the margins and those who are vulnerable, we can catch a glimpse of what Micah meant to love kindness and do justice.

At the same time, we must begin to wrench ourselves away from our comforts and idols. As we examine what it is that has a grip on our hearts, we can identify the natural obstacles to loving kindness and doing justice in our daily lives. For many of us, that will mean forcing ourselves to operate outside of our normal rhythms and comfort zones. But as we do this, we will not feel more constrained; instead we will feel more free. We were created to worship God, to walk with him through our lives. And true worship of God calls us "to do justice, and to love kindness" (**v 8**).

Questions for reflection

1. "The basic point here is that God is not pleased if we elevate one aspect of what he requires of us as his people, while ignoring the rest." Why is it so easy to excuse, or not even to notice, the elevation of just one aspect of what he requires?

2. How has your view of justice changed as a result of reading this section?

3. How can you reflect on the *hesed* shown to you at the cross in such a way that it will move you to do justice and love kindness?

PART TWO

The court of creation has been summoned and the defendants named (Micah 6:1-2); the standard has been set (v 8). Now follows the charge and verdict (**v 9-12**), and then the sentence (**v 13-16**).

The Charge

First, who is *bringing* the charge? **Verse 9**: "The voice of the LORD cries…"! Micah adds that it is wisdom to heed the sound of the Lord's voice with awe: to fear the LORD is the beginning of wisdom (Proverbs 1:7). Micah is saying that only a fool would shut their ears to what is about to be said.

Second, who is *hearing* the charge? "The city" (Micah 6:9)—that is, the capital city of Jerusalem; or, to put it another way, all the inhabitants who live without reference to the desire of the Lord for the city.

Third, what is the *content* of the charges?

- *Possession of unjustly procured treasures* (**v 10**). "Can I forget any longer the treasures of wickedness in the house of the wicked, and the scant measure that is accursed?" These people were involved in procuring treasures for themselves in unrighteous ways. God cannot forget or overlook these injustices. To do so would be de facto to bless them and therefore to make himself complicit in the injustice.

- *Using manipulative weights and measures* (**v 11**). "Shall I acquit the man with wicked scales and with a bag of deceitful weights?" In the ancient world, standardized measures were hard to establish, so trading was done on an honor system whereby people would use just weights and measures. These people were using unjust measures and weights. They were circumventing the honor system and deceitfully manipulating people's trust as they engaged in commerce.

■ *An underlying web of violence and deceit* (**v 12**). "Your rich men are full of violence; your inhabitants speak lies, and their tongue is deceitful in their mouth." They were essentially doing anything for personal gain, even if it meant adopting deceitful ways, or hurting people in the process. They weren't concerned about such things because ultimately their priority was personal gain.

The sentence comes in as the charge is read out, for the LORD assumes the roles of both impartial prosecutor and impartial judge. There is no question that Israel have been behaving in these ways. The only question is whether God should "forget" what they have been doing and "acquit" them. The verdict is guilty—will God pass sentence and if so, what will it be?

Calculating People

It is all too easy to read passages such as this and think subconsciously, "OK, but what does any of this have to do with me? My scales work fine!" We have to ask ourselves the question: in what ways do I aim to work the system for personal gain? We might not literally engage in dishonest manipulation of weights and scales and so on. But what's the modern-day equivalent? It is to manipulate our financial power, or our professional position, or our relationships, or even our religion for personal gain. Then we are guilty too: because why do we manipulate? Because we are calculating people, and our approach is that of a cost-benefit analysis.

We often see all of life in economic and transactional terms. Because we are brought up in a society that tells us we are consumers, we can tend to look at all of life through a commercial lens. In the various areas of our lives, we look at the ways in which we can get the greatest benefit with the smallest amount of investment. How can I minimize costs and maximize profit? The focus is on a self-derived gain, not on an other-oriented equality and justice. This, of course, has been the charge against the Israelites all along in the book of Micah.

Consider how we choose our careers, and decide whether to move jobs. Nathan Hatch, who is President of Wake Forest University, spoke in 2009 about how there is a disproportionate number of young adults crammed into the fields of finance, consulting, corporate law, and specialized medicine, because of the high salaries and the reputation that these professions bring. His concern was that they were choosing these professions not by asking the questions, "What job can I do that helps people to flourish? How can I seek what is good?" but by asking, "What job will help me flourish?" and "What makes me feel, or look, good?" (*Renewing the Wellsprings of Responsibility*, quoted in Timothy Keller, *Counterfeit Gods*, page 79). When we think this way—and it feels so natural, because it is the way of the Western world—we are not concerned about human flourishing; we are more concerned about which job will help us to flourish. This is what happens in an overly individualistic culture when the heart impulse is that of personal gain. It ultimately causes a consumeristic posture with regard to everything in life.

That's the charge—and it is against us as much as it is against Israel. At any point when you are willing to manipulate relationships, the market, or your reality (in the way you view yourself, others, or even God) because you are directed by cost-benefit analysis in order to maximize your own flourishing, you are guilty. It's manipulation caused by selfish calculation—it's sin. That is the charge.

The Sentence

"Therefore"—here is the sentence being handed down in response to the verdict—"I strike you with a grievous blow, making you desolate because of your sins" (**v 13**). The rod that is introduced here is used to strike a grievous blow. We might hear this and ask, "What kind of a God is this that he would strike them and bring this kind of grievous blow?" But this is not a fatal blow; God is not promising utter destruction. Yet he is saying that he will address the injustices of this world.

He will make desolate those things which have been created by sin. That is the sentence in broad terms.

The specific sentence is the nullification of Israel's manipulative self-focused way of life. They will eat without finding satisfaction or ending their hunger; they will save, but lose what they tried to preserve (**v 14**). God will not give them what they trampled on others in order to get. Paradoxically, in **God's economy**, he is saying that ultimately it is humility that leads to fulfillment. God is saying in **verse 15**, *I will ensure that you are laboring in vain. You're doing all the industrious work, but your work is not going to be productive. It's not going to bear fruit. You're not going to be able to find the joy and happiness of the work that you're involved in. I will not allow you to make this approach to life work well for you.*

Israel in Micah's day was being warned of invasion and exile. They would be separated from all they had worked to gain. They would leave all their savings behind. And, of course, the ultimate exile is death. Death forces us to leave everything behind and separates us from all we have accumulated. It is why those who lay up stores in barns but are not rich toward God are, in Jesus' estimation, fools (Luke 12:20).

One day, we will all have to face judgment. You can try to rationalize and explain your actions and life: "Oh, but this happened. Oh, but my parents didn't love me enough. Oh, but my husband was like this. Oh, but my work is like this." But whatever excuses we might give, ultimately we have to be honest. We are all exposed before the bar of justice. Instinctively we know that we're not as good as we ought to be. We know that we would rather pursue our own personal gain than be concerned about the needs of others. We might say, "My life is not as corrupt as the lives of these Israelites." But it's not a difference of kind; it's a difference of degree. The point the Bible makes over and over again, as it gives this very honest assessment of the human heart and of the human condition, is that ultimately we are all accountable before the bar of justice. Everyone must give an account.

And the sentence is a life of exile. We will not enjoy the fruits of our manipulative labors.

The Conviction Reversed

Verse 16 is basically a recapitulation of the whole passage. Omri and Ahab were particularly idolatrous kings of Israel (1 Kings 16:21 – 22:40). Because the people have kept their "statutes" and followed in their "works" and heeded "their counsels," God will, he tells them, "make you a desolation, and your inhabitants a hissing; so you shall bear the scorn of my people" (Micah **6:16**). God restates the charge, passes verdict, and gives sentence. But what is being added here is that it all comes back to idolatry. They have been receiving the counsel of the idolaters rather than listening to the counsel to walk with God and pursue justice. Now they face desolation and they face scorn. Is there any hope?

The gospel connection is not explicit here in our passage; that's why we're grateful that we don't have only this passage. There is a parallel passage in Isaiah, which is a similar period in history, at the same stage of the plot-line of God's plan to redeem his people. We find a similar warning of God's judgment on his people's sin, using similar language, in Isaiah 51:17-20. Then Isaiah 52 – 53 famously talks about the suffering servant—and of course Jesus is the fulfillment of that prophecy. Those verses in Isaiah 51 are the charges against and sentence upon Israel. After reading that, it elicits a similar response: "Is there any hope whatsoever at all for these people?" Then Isaiah 52 – 53 comes; we should listen to it in light of the sentence that has been issued to God's people.

God's servant is wise, and exalted. He is not like those around him, like those Micah and Isaiah have both issued God's charge against. Yet he was smitten by God. He was afflicted. He was wounded for their transgressions. He was crushed for their iniquities. He was oppressed, judged, cut off. This is the same language that is used earlier on in Micah 5:10-13 about how God's people would be cut off from their horses, cities, sorcerers, and carved images. God's servant was stricken for those transgressions as he bore the sin of many.

"You shall bear the scorn of my people" (Micah **6:16**). In order to reverse the indictment, someone else needs to bear the scorn of "my people." And he did.

All throughout Scripture, the judgment comes, the charge is given, but there's always a response from God himself where he is willing to address us. So take Isaiah 57:17-18: "Because of the iniquity of his unjust gain I was angry, I struck him; I hid my face and was angry, but he went on backsliding in the way of his own heart. I have seen his ways, but I will heal him..." The Lord knows that if no one else addresses this, then the people will have to bear the scorn of their own sins; they will be cut off for their idolatry. But God, in the person of Jesus his servant, reverses the verdict on us by taking our sentence for us. When we read the famous verses of Isaiah 52 – 53 in the context of Isaiah 51:17-20 and Micah 6—and when we understand that we sit in the same courtroom and hear the same verdict and sentence as Israel in those prophets' day—then we grow a deeper sense of awe and have a greater sense of his bearing our scorn.

Knowing the Verdict

What difference does the verdict and the sentence make in us every day? Everyone has a sense of being on trial and needing to know the verdict. We look for a verdict every day. We want people to assess our lives (or to self-assess our own lives) and enjoy the kind of positive verdict that we desire and strive for.

The Bible tells us that there is a more crucial verdict, for our lives are being lived in a courtroom before the presence of a holy God. The Bible says that we cannot justify ourselves; but that someone else has come and justified us by their actions. The ultimate verdict has been given, and it is that someone was willing to be afflicted, wounded, crushed, oppressed, judged, cut off, and stricken, and to bear the sins of our self-gain. The ultimate verdict is that because Jesus went all through this and bore our sentence, "there is therefore now no condemnation for those who are in Christ Jesus" (Romans 8:1). We already know the verdict on us at the beginning of each day—before we even do anything, good or bad, in our day.

So we don't have to go out into the world thinking that we are on trial. We don't need to perform in order to get a positive verdict, or to measure and calibrate our worth. We don't need to manipulate others or calculate how we can achieve our own flourishing. The ultimate verdict has already been pronounced. We are who we are because of what Jesus Christ has done on our behalf. He has borne our sins in himself; he stood in our place so that we can get this declaration. This leads to a life

> We don't have to go out into the world thinking that we are on trial.

that is free: one that pursues the gain of others and glorifies God; a life that is lived for his cause, and not concerned about our ability or self-gain.

The apostle Paul understood this, and so he said, "To live is Christ, and to die is gain" (Philippians 1:21). His life was restructured and reorganized in a completely different way, since death no longer meant losing everything but gaining everything. And so he could say, "Whatever gain I had, I counted as loss for the sake of Christ … For his sake I … count [or, we might say, "calculate"] them as rubbish, in order that I may gain Christ and be found in him" (Philippians 3:7, 8b-9). Can you see that this is absolutely the opposite of what drove Israel in Micah's day, and what naturally drives us in ours?

We have no more reason to walk around in fear. The gospel tells us that God already knows that we are all frauds. We cannot hide the truth from him. But we do not need to. The charge and sentence have been absorbed, and the court adjourned, and we're free to go.

Questions for reflection

1. Did the idea of operating out of a "cost-benefit analysis" challenge you in any way? How?

2. Have you experienced the truth that it is humility that leads to fulfillment?

3. Do you ever live feeling that you need to perform to merit God's positive verdict? Or that you need to hear a positive verdict from someone other than God (and if so, who)? How can Romans 8:1 change the way you feel and live?

9. RECOVERING THE LOST ART OF LAMENT

Until now, we have walked and traveled with this prophet over very tough terrain. And now we see here at the start of the final chapter of his book that Micah is personally processing what he sees. He is deeply affected on an emotional and existential level by what he is observing: his people torn apart by their own doing; his society unraveling; his God warning of judgment and exile before restoration. Here is God's prophet, responding to an almost unimaginably difficult situation.

This leads us to ask: How does God want us to deal with the great difficulties of life? Does he want us to ignore them, to get over them, to power through them, or to be crushed by them? Following Micah, we will see that God actually invites his people to lament over them. He wants us to honestly assess what we're seeing, and also to pour out our great sorrow to him at what we see.

The Reality of Lament

What is lament? Lament is a passionate expression of grief and sorrow. To lament is to mourn, to grieve, to beat one's breast in anguish. A lament is not whining, complaining, griping, or grumbling. Certainly a lament is not trivial, trite, petty, or superficial. Micah shows us what it means to lament when he says, "Woe is me!" (Micah **7:1**): *What misery is mine.* This is a classic phrase in Scripture that introduces a formal lament. Unfortunately, for many of us, even Christians in the church, when we see the expression "Woe is me!" we tend to think that it sounds like a selfish pity party. "Woe is me! No one loves me. Why are my life circumstances so challenging? No one listens to me. Woe is me!" But in Scripture, "Woe is me!" is one of the most powerful and deeply felt phrases that can be invoked. It sums up the feeling of a grieving mother who has lost a child, or of a widow or widower facing their spouse's funeral, or of a conquered nation. "Woe is me!" is only used in the most dire, grim, ruinous circumstances.

> "Woe is me!" is one of the most powerful phrases that can be invoked.

Through the rest of **verse 1**, Micah uses an agricultural image to explain his experience; the image is of a vinedresser who goes to his plants to collect the fruit. He sees that though it is harvest-time everything has been picked clean, and so there is no fruit to eat. There is no fig to desire. Why? Because, "the great man utters the evil desire of his soul" (**v 3**). *Because evil powerful men are going after their own desires,* Micah says, *I'm left with nothing to fulfill my need* (**v 1**). The people are being picked clean. Lament expresses a state of existential bankruptcy and a state of intense emptiness when we have no recourse—no way of explaining or understanding what is happening around us. Have you felt that way, when you don't have the words to explain your experience? That's where Micah is.

The Bible is not ashamed of lament. In the Psalms, 60 of the 150 are categorized as lament psalms—40%. The prophets lament as well. Look at Jeremiah, often known as the "weeping prophet." There is one book in the Bible that is devoted to laments, and it is aptly named Lamentations. Why does the Bible embrace a lament? Because it is honest about human experience. It doesn't settle for some superficially shallow way of describing what's going on, as if to pretend that suffering is not serious or that it is just an illusion. We, too, must learn to meaningfully and honestly express the anguish of our hearts, if we are to avoid superficiality or pretense. The Bible deals with real life. Christianity does not ignore the wounds of the world; it draws near to them. It acknowledges suffering and pain.

Modern Christianity has difficulty understanding and appreciating the discipline of lament. Yet as Emmanuel Katongole and Chris Rice have written:

"The first language of the church in a deeply broken world [should not be] strategy, but prayer." (*Reconciling All Things*, page 77)

Here is what Martin Luther King Jr. wrote at his kitchen table in Montgomery when yet he had received yet another death threat:

"Lord, I'm down here trying to do what's right, but Lord I must confess that I'm weak now. I'm faltering. I'm losing my courage. Now I am afraid. I'm at the end of my powers. I have nothing left. I've come to the point where I cannot face it alone."

(Quoted in *Reconciling All Things*, page 77, footnote 1)

This is biblical, and healthy; it's the attitude which enables a person to lament.

This is something beautiful that we can learn from the African American tradition, in which many were being torn apart by slavery as they cried their laments. These were real laments:

"Sometimes I feel like a motherless child a long way from home. Sometimes I feel like I'm almost gone, a long way from home."

(*Reconciling All Things*, page 77)

Lament and hope co-exist in African-American spirituals in a way that is very biblical and that most of us need to learn from. It is very biblical because in the Psalms, we find psalms of praise *and* psalms of lament. They are found together because our own human experience shows that sometimes we're singing and sometimes we're crying.

"A lament is not despair. The lament is a cry directed to God … It is the cry of those who see the truth of the world's deep ruptures and wounds and the cost of seeking peace."

(*Reconciling All Things*, page 78)

In a very real sense, in our modern Western world, we need to slow the pace of life in order to consider, to listen, and to lament for ourselves or for others. Are you slowing down to make the space and the time in your life to be able to hear the crying? Or is everything so speedy that you don't have the capacity to hear, so you end up being indifferent to all that's unraveling around you or possibly in you?

Reasons for Lament

Before we see what causes Micah to lament as he does, it is worth asking ourselves: what would cause me to cry out, "Woe is me"? What is, literally, lamentable to me? Another way of asking this is by posing the question: what is it that I can't imagine losing in my life? Or what, if I lost it, would cause me to feel there was no meaning in my life? Some of our answers to those questions are valid things, such as the loss of a loved one, the disintegration of our family, or the loss of personal security and wellbeing. But what we grieve can oftentimes reveal the things that have an idolatrous grip on our lives. Would my world fall apart if my retirement did not go according to my plan? If my investments were to collapse? If I lost my job? If I never enjoy the type of relationship I have dreamed of? Or if I never achieve recognition and applause in my education, or career, or parenting?

What are the reasons why Micah grieves? There are three of them, and they all have two things in common: they are about the good of others and they are about the glory of God.

The first reason Micah grieves is because of the disappearance of the righteous. "The godly has perished from the earth, and there is no one upright among mankind; they all lie in wait for blood, and each hunts the other with a net" (**v 2**). When he said in **verse 1** that he found "no first-ripe fig that my soul desires," it turns out that Micah was speaking about the godly and the righteous in that way. He was saying that good fruit—righteousness—was nowhere for him to enjoy. Further, what he does see is fruitlessness (**v 4**): "The best of them is like a brier, the most upright of them a thorn hedge." The best of the people are a thorn hedge: fruitless, and painful.

When human beings align themselves to God's desires, then the community thrives. This is something that you don't need to be a Christian to appreciate: that people who are loving one another is better than people who are hating one another. Communities thrive when people are willing to die to themselves and not get people to orbit around them; when people are willing to sacrifice whatever resources they have for the common good.

Micah next uses a very strange image of each person hunting another with a net (**v 2**). He's not saying that there is some sort of cannibalistic activity going on here; it's simply an image to say that some people prey upon other people. They want to subdue other people for personal gain. They want to be able to get what they desire at the expense of others who are also pursuing what they desire, or indeed pursuing the very minimum that they need. This is the reason for the lament: the lack of the knowledge of God. Notice that the lack of that knowledge is evidenced in community breakdown.

> The lack of the knowledge of God is evidenced in community breakdown.

The second reason for Micah's lament is the corruption of leaders and their peace-keeping structures. "Their hands are on what is evil, to do it well; the prince and the judge ask for a bribe, and the great man utters the evil desire of his soul; thus they weave it together" (**v 3**). There are three leaders (or types of leadership) here, each of whom have been given the responsibility of stewarding their authority in order to care responsibly for the people whom God has entrusted into their hands. One is a prince, one is a judge, and one is this great man. They're asked to weave peace into the structure of the community. They're supposed to be peace-weavers, weavers of shalom… but they have become obstructers of justice. What they weave together is evil, and they do it well. Again, the best of the leaders is a thorn hedge (**v 4**).

Whenever we see this in our own context, we are supposed to grieve. We're supposed to grieve over corrupt leaders, over those who do not execute justice when they could. We are supposed to grieve when the leaders are not concerned about those who are in need. It's an occasion for lament.

The third reason why Micah laments is the tearing of the social fabric. "Put no trust in a neighbor; have no confidence in a friend; guard the doors of your mouth from her who lies in your arms; for the son treats the father with contempt, the daughter rises up against her mother, the daughter-in-law against her mother-in-law; a man's enemies are the men of his own house" (**v 5-6**). This is a complete social unraveling. Neighbors cannot be trusted, friends are unworthy of confidence, and family life is no better: spouses are emotionally estranged from one another, sons line up against fathers, and daughters rebel against their mothers. This is not an introductory lesson on how to relate to in-laws. The problems go much deeper than that. "A man's enemies are the men of his own house." Every man and every woman is for himself or herself. This is what is lamentable.

We are being shown that it is right to lament, and we are being shown what to lament over. When we are honest, we realize that so much of our lamenting concerns only ourselves and our thwarted dreams or desires; at best, it may extend to the interests of our household. But when was the last time you lamented over the lack of godliness around you; or the corruption in the leaders over you; or the tearing of social fabric in your community? All too often we are indifferent when it comes to these things. We should not be. God created a world of shalom; it is a matter of grief that that is not the world we currently see. If we will not weep over it, we shall never really know the joy of the prospect of its restoration when its Master returns.

Questions for reflection

1. Having read this section, how would you define "lament"?

2. How do you respond to the questions at the top of page 134?

3. If you struggle to know joy over God's restoration of people and his world, to what extent might this be because you are not lamenting ungodliness and corruption in this world?

PART TWO

Hope in Lament

If we look around and acknowledge all the reasons to grieve—the disappearance of righteousness, the corruption of leaders, and the tearing of the social fabric—how are we supposed to respond?

Some of us are overwhelmed because we live in a digital age, in which we receive an overwhelming amount of information. We get all the alerts and notifications, and we read headlines of terrible things happening in the world. And in order not to be overwhelmed, we slowly become indifferent to these things. Instead, we then begin to check to see what our friends are saying or doing on social media. There grows in us a complacency to what is happening around us. The only other option seems to be crushing despair, and we don't want to go there.

What does Micah do? He hopes in his lament: "But as for me, I will look to the LORD; I will wait for the God of my salvation; my God will hear me" (**v 7**). We can break this down into three actions: he looks, he waits, and then he trusts.

There is a really interesting passage in Luke 7:1-10 that gives us a picture of this. Here we have an episode involving a Roman centurion; he's a high official, like a major or a colonel, in the Roman army. He obviously has many soldiers under his authority, but he has a servant whom he greatly values, and this servant is sick and about to die (v 2). This officer sends a delegation to represent him and to go and plead on his behalf, asking Jesus to come and help—and this delegation is made up of "elders of the Jews" (v 3). But the Romans were not supposed to have Jewish friends, and the Jews did not have Roman friends. The Romans were Gentiles; not only that, they were the oppressors who used their power to subjugate the Jews. So the fact that he is able to send a delegation of the elders of the Jews means that he is highly respected by the Jewish authorities. He has presumably interacted with them in honest ways, caring for them in their plight, so that when he asks them to go see Jesus on his behalf, they are willing to go. The narrative says that they went to Jesus and pleaded with him and earnestly asked him. This is what they said about the centurion: "He is worthy to have you do this for him, for he loves our nation, and he is the one who built us our synagogue" (v 4-5).

They appear to be working out of a **moralistic** framework; so they make this centurion seem very worthy by telling Jesus all the things he has done for them, because that means that he therefore deserves Jesus' favor. The text doesn't tell us what Jesus says in response—but he goes with the elders of the Jews over to the centurion's house, where his servant is sick and about to die. Then while Jesus is on his way, not very far off from this soldier's home, the centurion sends another delegation of representatives to speak on his behalf. Why? Because he knows that "I am not worthy to have you come under my roof. Therefore I did not presume to come to you" (v 6-7). He doesn't presume anything. The elders of the Jews have said that he's worthy, but he's saying, *No, I'm not worthy. I don't presume that you should come, that you should waste your time in coming into my house.*

The centurion is humble. He just asks Jesus to "say the word, and let my servant be healed. For I too am a man set under authority, with soldiers under me: and I say to one, 'Go,' and he goes; and to another, 'Come,' and he comes; and to my servant, 'Do this,' and he does it" (v 7-8).

Jesus responds to this by marveling at him and then healing his servant, telling his followers that "not even in Israel have I found such faith" (v 9). But let's ask: how did the centurion get to that point? How was he able to look, to wait, and to trust so that Jesus marveled and said that there was no one in Israel who had faith like this Gentile, this Roman centurion? The centurion was essentially saying, *I'm a man of great authority, but I am going to view myself as a servant, just as I tell my servants to do whatever they need to do because I have authority. If you tell me to do whatever you want me to do, I will submit to your authority.*

Do you see what he is doing? He is looking to Jesus. He is waiting for Jesus. And he is trusting Jesus. He doesn't act as if he deserves anything from Jesus. But he still humbly trusts that Jesus is both able and willing to do what he needs. He knows that Jesus can reverse his cause for lament by healing his highly valued servant. So he puts himself under Jesus' authority and says, *I deserve nothing from you, but I look to you to reverse this crisis, because I know who you are and I trust you.*

Looking, Waiting, and Trusting

But the centurion, though he had the greatest faith Jesus had yet found in Israel, is not the most wonderful example of looking, waiting, and trusting that we find in the Gospels. That is because Micah was not the last prophet to look at Jerusalem and lament—for we see in Luke 19:41-42 that Jesus wept over Jerusalem, and for the same reasons as Micah. "And when he drew near and saw the city, he wept over it, saying, 'Would that you, even you, had known on this day the things that make for peace! But now they are hidden from your eyes.'" Jesus offered his lamenting cries. Hebrews 5:7 tells us that, "In the days of his flesh, Jesus offered up prayers and supplications, with loud cries and tears, to him who was able to save him from death, and he was heard because of his reverence." Jesus looked, he waited, and he trusted in God.

This leads us to the cross, where we see the ultimate display of Jesus' looking, waiting, and trusting in God. On the cross, we can hear Jesus' cry of lament: "My God, my God, why have you forsaken me?" (Mark 15:34; Psalm 22:1). Notice here that Jesus didn't utter, "My bones, my bones..." or "My garments, my garments..." He did not cry out for a physical remedy. What he did cry out for was the nearness of God. He cried out for his presence.

But where was God? Where was God's fatherly care? Could he not have rescued his Son, or have come close to him? Was Jesus looking and waiting and trusting in the wrong place? The Father's silence was, of course, not an indication of his inability. He certainly could have done everything that would be natural for a father to do for his crying child. But he chose not to act. Father and Son both knew what needed to be done. Jesus had to go through this guilt-bearing process for people who were too blind to see their need for it and who, even when they would start to see their desperate situation, would not have the ability to save themselves. For this, the Father and Jesus experienced the reality of the separation that we face eternally. For this, Jesus cried out the most heartrending lament in all of history.

It's imperative that we understand the weight of this separation. Many of us know what it is to feel anxiety as we anticipate or experience a separation. What causes anxiety over that separation, when we feel no anxiety about other separations? It is the depth of the relationship

> Jesus cried out the most heartrending lament in all of history.

that you are being distanced from, and the length of time that you have been together with the other person. That is what causes the pain that you endure when separation comes. The greater the depth of the bond and the longer the time you have spent together, the worse the parting is. Scripture tells us that God the Father and God the Son were together in perfect unity, enjoying each other's company and love, for eternity. Imagine the pain that comes in severing a bond like this! And yet, they both knew that this would have to be done if sin was to be judged *and* sinners were to be justified. And they were both willing for it to be done.

This place where Jesus experienced forsakenness—this place of ultimate lament—is where we need to come when we are lamenting. When we cry out to God for his help, we can look to the cross and know that God will not turn his back on us. God's rejection is what Jesus has already experienced, in our place. Jesus' prayer for his Father's nearness was rejected so that we can know that our prayers seeking nearness to him will never be rejected.

Never forget that Jesus was willing to experience infinite cosmic upheaval and separation—hell—as the cup of God's wrath was essentially stirred under his own nostrils and as he drank it down to the last dregs. In Gethsemane, Jesus was asked, in effect, this question: *Are you going to continue with this and absorb the wrath of God for these people who fail you all the time? Are you going to move forward and do this for them?* And Jesus said *Yes* (Mark 14:35-36). Since Jesus faced death, hell, separation, and wrath, and he did not give up on us, why then would we think that he would give up on us now? Why would we think that he'd get to a point where he would say, *I made a mistake in dying for them?* If the cup did not make him give up on us, then nothing else will.

> Since Jesus faced wrath and he did not give up on us, why would we think he would give up on us now?

We need to let this truth of what Jesus has done for us melt our hearts and cause us to wait, to look, to slow down, to process, and to lament ourselves. We lament in a confident sadness, knowing that our prayers will be heard because Jesus' prayer of, "My God, my God, why have you forsaken me?" was not heard. Through the cross, we are invited to run to our Father to let out our cries of lament. Because of Jesus, we can know that our lament is heard. As we lament, we know how much God went out of his way, even to the point of rejecting the cries of his Son and willingly experiencing a separation that we cannot comprehend, to draw close to us and draw us close to him. We can cry our laments in hope, knowing that we cry to a Father who will never turn his face away. We must let it sink deep in our hearts that our lamenting has a legitimate place in God's heart because of Jesus, the One who experienced the ultimate rejection and the pain of unimaginable separation on our behalf. And so, whatever the cause of our lament—and there will be many, and they will cut deep—we always can say to ourselves, to others, and to God:

"As for me, *I will look* to the LORD;
   I will wait for the God of my salvation;
   My God will hear me." (Micah **7:7**; emphasis mine)

Questions for reflection

As and when you lament, how will you…

1. look?

2. wait?

3. trust?

10. WHO IS LIKE GOD?

By the time we reach the second half of Micah 7 and read once more of God's judgment, we might be tempted to say, "OK, I get it. God is a holy God. He's bringing judgment; he is a just God. Can we just move on?" But Micah has not yet "moved on," and neither should we. We have to talk about this because Scripture talks about this; but we also have to talk about this because we actually want to believe in a God who stands for justice. We want a God who actually will do something about the injustices in the world; who will look upon the unjust acts and trample on them, because he is opposed to all the attempts to vandalize the harmony and health of his people.

God loves peace; he loves shalom. We want a God of justice; our problem is that we don't want him to be just toward us. We are pleased that God is opposed to sin generally, but not that he is opposed to my sin specifically, nor that he refuses to tolerate my attempts to redefine what sin is. We want a God of justice, but we resist the notion of a God of justice.

The last few verses of chapter 7 not only state that God is a holy and just God, but also once more inject a vision of hope that we so desperately long to hear. The heart of the conclusion to Micah is this: vindicating justice is coming to, and for, God's people. God is not ultimately going to overlook their sin, yet the remnant of his inheritance—those who have been the recipients (as well as perpetrators) of unjust acts, oppression, idolatry, and the misuse of power—will be raised up in a way that does not undermine the justice of God. God has plans for his people beyond judgment.

No Room to Gloat

In 7:1-7, we saw a beautiful picture of what it means to lament over the oppression and the injustices of society, and over one's own idolatry and the pursuit of selfish gain. Micah was grieved at the state of his nation and with God's people. In essence, what he's doing here in **verse 8** is to turn to the enemies of God—the Assyrians, who were oppressing Israel in the 8th century BC—and say, *I don't want you to gloat or to think that you ultimately have the upper hand. I don't want you to think that God has abandoned his people and that you can laugh at with impunity as you take us into exile.* Israel fell in 722 BC, and they were brought into captivity under the Assyrian rule. The southern kingdom of Judah would fall to Babylon in 587 BC. But God had already said that this was not the end of the story, either for his people or for their enemies.

Micah warns "my enemy" to "rejoice not over me," for "when I fall, I shall rise" (**v 8**). Why? Because "the LORD will be a light to me." After the downfall, there will be an uprising; after the darkness, there will be light. "Then my enemy will see, and shame will cover her who said to me, 'Where is the LORD your God?' My eyes will look upon her; now she will be trampled down like the mire of the streets" (**v 10**). These enemies will have their day mocking God and mocking God's people: *Where is the Lord your God? Is he on your side? He doesn't seem to be present if he's allowing all of this to happen to his people.* Micah is saying on behalf of God that that day will not continue forever. Shame will cover the enemies of God, not the people of God. They will be trampled down. Vindication is coming on behalf of God's people.

Verses 11-13 paint a glorious picture of restoration beyond judgment. There will come "a day for the building of your walls! In that day the boundary shall be far extended. In that day they will come to you … from sea to sea and from mountain to mountain. But the earth will be desolate because of its inhabitants, for the fruit of their deeds." Micah is talking again about how God is going to speak and act against the enemies of God. In **verses 14-17**, God makes himself clear: the other nations will be in awe of Israel as well, just as they were "in the days of old" (**v 14**) "when you came out of the land of Egypt" (**v 15**). Those who caused Israel to quake will find that now "they shall be in fear of you" (**v 17**). At the same time, though, God promises that "the boundary shall be far extended" (**v 11**). There will be a remnant of God's inheritance that will even come from those enemy nations, not only from the nation of Israel (**v 12**). There's always this tension in Scripture: judgment and justice are coming upon the oppression, the injustices, and the idolatry—but at the same time, there will be a remnant which God will preserve, whom he will consider as his people. Blessing will come to the faithful remnant of God's ancient people, sinful and undeserving as they are; blessing will come to some from the other nations too, sinful and undeserving as they also are. The promise to Abram in Genesis 12:3 relies on God's grace, not on humanity's merit. For those whom God will call, defeat is not the end of the story.

These verses should help us when we experience difficulties; it is not evidence that God has abandoned us. He never leaves or forsakes his people in the midst of the darkness. It is not evidence that God is powerless to help us. It may very well be that God allows the trials and difficulties in our lives to demonstrate that he is with us because he disciplines those he loves, and he shields those he has saved—not from trials, but from faithlessness (Hebrews 12:3-11; 1 Peter 1:5-7). Deliverance and salvation will come to God's people.

Again, Micah is teaching us to hold justice and wrath together with deliverance and grace. This is not easy to do; but it is essential, as well as being biblical. In an article entitled "The Compassionate Truth about Judgment," the pastor Scott Sauls says that the idea of heaven is easy to embrace, but the ideas of hell, wrath, justice, and judgment

> For those whom God will call, defeat is not the end of the story.

are not. But, he says, the doctrine of judgment is in fact compassion-ate. How? Imagine if we dismiss the doctrine of God's judgment. Then all the victims of injustice, violence, and oppression have no hope. If this all-powerful God doesn't bring judgment for the injustices, the oppression, and the misuse of power, then all that victims are left with is the injustice and exploitation and manipulation they suffer at the hands of their fellow humans (http://bit.ly/2eSSHvq; accessed 9/8/17).

If there is no ultimate accounting for evil, then what do you say to the Jews about Hitler? What do you say to the little girl who was sold into the sex trade by greedy, oppressive, wicked men? What do you say to the boy who was abused by his father? What human message, never mind Christian message, would you be able to give to that individual?

It actually makes little sense to say, "I don't want a wrathful God; I just want a loving, merciful, and gracious God." But if God is loving, then he must surely be angry about evil. God's loving wrath is actually tied very closely with our value and worth as human beings. If you have some deity that does not demonstrate wrath or justice—if he is only ever loving and gracious without any judgment—then actually you are of little value to that god. That god does not care enough about you to care about what others do to you; he doesn't care enough about your own integrity and humanity to care about what you do to others. And that god has never shown you how valued you are because he's never given anything up for you. The God of the Bible cares enough to judge you and to save you, at unimaginable cost to himself.

C.S. Lewis, in one of his essays in *Letters to Malcolm*, writes an open letter to Malcolm. Malcolm has trouble, like most 20th and 21st-century Western people, with the idea of a God who gets angry. He finds it more helpful to think of God's power and wrath and justice and judgment like a live electrical wire. There's power there, and if you go and touch it, you're going to be harmed. It's not a personal, conscious anger. Malcolm says, "The live wire doesn't feel angry with us, but if we blunder against it, we get a shock." Lewis responds:

"My dear Malcolm, what do you suppose you have gained by sub-stituting the image of a live wire for that of an angered majesty? You have shut us all up in despair; for the angry can forgive, and electricity can't … Turn God's wrath into mere enlightened disapproval, and you also turn His love into mere humanitarian-ism. The 'consuming fire' and the 'perfect beauty' both vanish. We have, instead, a judicious headmistress or a conscientious magistrate." (*Letters to Malcolm*, pages 96-97)

If our conception of God is that he's simply a God of love, and not that he's a God of love *and* justice, then we will never know that we're truly valued, and we can never know that there will be justice.

If a judging God does not exist, then all we have is the chaos and the disintegration that we see. In his article, Scott Sauls goes on to say that for love to truly be love, there must be judgment. If there is no judgment, then there is no hope for the slave, the rape victim, the child who has been abused or bullied, and so on. If nobody is called to account before a cosmic judgment seat for violence and oppression, then the victims will never see justice and the guilty will get off scot-free. We need a God who gets angry, righteously angry, over injustice. We need a God who will protect his children, who will once and for all remove bullies and perpetrators of evil from his world. That is what we need. We need a God who is holy and just. We need a holy God who is going to come and obliterate the injustices in the world. Wonder-fully Micah, along with the rest of the Scriptures, assures us that this is exactly what God is like.

Bearing the Indignation

God's vindicating justice had implications for God's people, Israel, be-cause God's people were sinners too. That was the whole reason that their enemies would be allowed by God—even used by God—to in-vade, as we saw back in Micah 1:10-16. Again, Micah reminds us that the heavenly courtroom trial does not simply go away. Micah prob-ably wrote most of this before the people went into exile in 722 BC.

And he promises that "I [as a member of the people] will bear the indignation of the LORD because I have sinned against him" (**7:9**). We have a holy God who will not overlook sin. One of the primary tensions in Scripture is how this just God can also be the God of **verse 18**: "Who is a God like you, pardoning iniquity … ?" How can the God of judgment upon iniquity also be the God who pardons iniquity?

As we have seen, Micah's very name means "Who is like God?" And no one is like God. No one is like this God, who can be a just God but also be a merciful God. But the tension remains: how can he both deal with sin and embrace the sinner? How can he root out injustice without destroying us, who are complicit in that injustice? It is the tension that runs right through the Old Testament (and indeed through most of the narrative laid out in the Gospels). Take, for instance, the way God reveals his glory, his character, to Moses in Exodus 34:6-7:

> "The LORD, the LORD, a God merciful and gracious, slow to anger, and abounding in steadfast love and faithfulness, keeping steadfast love for thousands, forgiving iniquity and transgression and sin, but who will by no means clear the guilty, visiting the iniquity of the fathers on the children and the children's children, to the third and the fourth generation."

When people memorize this portion of Scripture, they usually leave out that last portion—because they don't know what to do with it. They just want to believe that God is a pardoning God who passes over transgression.

> God is not only a God who is merciful, but a God who is majestic.

Again, we see a picture of a God who is not only a pardoning God, but who is also perfect, holy, and just. Not only a God who is merciful, but a God who is also majestic; not only a God who is willing to demonstrate humility, but a God who is also radically holy. That is the primary tension in Scripture. And that is a tension that we need to feel. We need to understand that we should not be acquitted, because we are guilty. It should not be a surprise that a loving God would judge, but it should be a surprise that he would find a way to forgive.

Questions for reflection

1. What do you make of the idea that judgment is compassionate?

2. "The promise to Abram in Genesis 12:3 relies on God's grace, not on humanity's merit." Why is this good news for each of us personally? What causes you to forget it?

3. Re-read the line above these questions for reflection. Does this truth surprise you? Should it? Why/why not, do you think?

PART TWO

Desperate for Jesus

Micah hints at how this great tension will be resolved: "I will bear the indignation of the LORD because I have sinned against him, until he pleads my cause and executes judgment for me" (Micah **7:9**). Again, this passage invokes the imagery of us being in the courtroom, on trial. We know we are constantly in the courtroom of public opinion; that's why, outside of rooting our identity in knowing Christ, we're so often stressed and anxious. But Micah is speaking of the heavenly courtroom. And, he says, the judge who should find him guilty will also be the One who pleads Micah's cause and "executes judgment *for* me" (my italics)—not, despite Micah's own sin, against "me."

We are being pointed to Jesus. We are being made desperate for Jesus. We are being led to the cross, where, because God went on trial and bore our judgment in our place, God's justice is satisfied and the court is adjourned and we walk free. God came and took our place, and bore our punishment, "so that he might be just and the justifier of the one who has faith in Jesus" (Romans 3:26).

Jesus is the one who is full of majesty and is just; but at the same time, he is willing to show us mercy because he justifies us through his atoning work on the cross and through his life and resurrection.

Micah couldn't have known how God would resolve the tension—but he trusts God and knows that he will. So he appeals to the character of the Judge. Look at Micah **7:18-20**:

"Who is a God like you, pardoning iniquity and passing over transgression for the remnant of his inheritance? He does not retain his anger forever, because he delights in steadfast love. He will again have compassion on us; he will tread our iniquities underfoot. You will cast all our sins into the depths of the sea. You will show faithfulness to Jacob and steadfast love to Abraham, as you have sworn to our fathers from the days of old."

Micah is showing us that God will keep his promises, and will pardon his people; his steadfast love will not run dry; he will remove his people's sins. Micah appeals to the Judge and says, in effect, *I know you will punish us, your people, because you are a God of justice. But I also know you have promised to forgive us, to remove our sins, and to delight in loving us. I don't know how you'll do this, but I do know that you will.*

We, living this side of Jesus' death, have the privilege of reading Micah in light of the cross. Look at **verses 8-10** from the perspective of Jesus. "Rejoice not over me, O my enemy" (**v 8**). Though hell rejoiced over the defeat of Jesus, it was premature. The death of Christ was followed by his resurrection. Jesus bore the indignation and wrath of God for our sins.

Then comes this wonderful **verse 9**: "I will bear the indignation of the LORD because I have sinned against him, until he pleads my cause and executes judgment for me." We see that God the Son was born and lived and died and rose and ascended so that he could plead our cause for us, for he has borne the indignation we deserved. That's why he went through hell on the cross. That's why he went into exile as he hung in the darkness. So we are people who know that we should bear his indignation, but instead we receive his forgiveness. He should speak against us, but instead he speaks for us.

> We are not just bold, but we are never just broken.

There's an interesting article and sermon on **verses 7-9** by John Piper, entitled "When I Fall, I Will Rise," in which he speaks about "bold brokenness" (desiringgod.org/messages/when-i-fall-i-will-rise, accessed 9/11/2017). Another way to say that would be "confident contrition" or "rugged remorse." Piper effectively says that if we read **verse 9** in the light of what Christ did on the cross, knowing how the tension has been resolved in Jesus, then the implication for us is that we will live with a bold brokenness. We are not just bold—self-confident, self-reliant, self-justifying; but we are never just broken—

crushed and timid and anxious. The tension here is that there will be both a boldness and a brokenness. There will be a confidence and also a contrite heart at the same time.

Piper goes on to say we will be "broken under indignation and bold in his grace." I think that we tend to separate the two, depending on where we are in our understanding. If we don't have confidence in our union with Christ, in the verdict that has already been declared, then we will only be bold to the degree that we're performing well enough. We will be broken to the degree that we're not performing well. We will never be able to have this paradoxical experience in our Christian life of a bold brokenness or a confident contrition; it'll one or the other. We tend to separate the two, but the Bible tells us here in **verse 9** that you can't separate them. "I will bear the indignation of the Lord because *I have sinned against him*, until *he pleads my cause* and executes judgment for me" (my italics). We know that the tension has been resolved because of **verse 18**: "Who is a God like you, pardoning iniquity and passing over transgression for the remnant of [your] inheritance?"

Boldness, Brokenness, and How to Love Others

One way that we can apply this is in our relationships with others (remember, Micah 1 – 3 showed us that wrong worship of a false god spills over into how we treat others; so knowing and worshiping the God of justice and grace will likewise show itself in how we treat others).

Oftentimes we get into an unhealthy cycle as we relate to people. The cycle will go something like this: You sin against someone; then the other person gets hurt; then after a few hours, depending on how complex the relationship is, you will come forward and maybe begrudgingly or out of duty say simply, "I'm sorry." Then the other person half-heartedly says, "It's okay." Then you pretend that nothing happened while worrying that they are holding it against you, and seeking to make up for it in some way, and so you read their behavior toward you in terms of whether they are punishing you.

There is never a real admission of sin, nor a real extension of forgiveness. We get stuck.

When we get into this cycle, we start to excuse our behavior even as we apologize for it. Imagine a husband who comes to his wife and says, "I'm sorry that you got so upset that I got angry." She responds by saying, "That's okay. I guess I'm really stressed because I had a long day at work." Can you see how unhealthy that is? Do you see what happened here? The husband, when he says that, is actually blaming his wife for his yelling. He says, "I'm sorry that you got so upset when I yelled at you." He is, at least in part, blaming her by saying, "You're just too sensitive. If you weren't that sensitive, then we wouldn't be in this situation." So he is planting the blame on his wife rather than in his own heart. He thinks that the ultimate problem is outside of himself and not inside of himself. Her response is then actually excusing him for his yelling, and also excusing herself. She blames her over-sensitivity on the length of the day: "The long day got to me." The problem here is being defined not as the husband worshiping an idol (maybe of comfort, or of power, or something else) in his heart; the ultimate problem here has become the length of the day. Again, sin is not being really confessed, and forgiveness is not being fully offered. We get stuck.

We can easily get our children stuck as well. We instruct them to say "sorry." Or we condition them by asking, "What are the magic words?" They quickly learn "please," "thank you," and "I'm sorry." These become like a get-me-out-of-jail card. By reciting them, everything is magically good again. They're let off the hook by simply saying, "I didn't mean it, but I said the magical word." Sin is not really being confessed, nor forgiveness really sought. Our kids get stuck with this skin-deep, say-the-right-thing mentality that doesn't touch their hearts.

Now think about **7:9**. Micah is saying, *I have sinned. I really did. I am not blaming my circumstances, God; nor am I blaming you* (which humans have tended to do since Adam did it, Genesis 3:12). Micah is saying, *I have sinned, and I am appealing to your gracious character and I am asking for forgiveness—for you to bear the cost of putting your indignation away, so that our relationship can be fully restored.*

And, at the cross, we find God's ultimate answer: *Yes. As I promised, I will forgive you for I have borne my own indignation. I have come and borne the judgment.*

And this is the way we break the cycle in which our human relationships get stuck. We learn to completely, unreservedly confess sin to each other from our hearts; we learn to bear the cost of putting away our right to be angry when we are sinned against, and to completely forgive and move on.

Who is a God Like Him?

How can we look at injustice and hate it, and want to fight against it? How can we be merciful to those who are in need? How can we forgive those people who harm us? How can we do all three of these things, consistently? There is only one way, and it is to believe in this God, who pardons iniquity and passes over transgression (Micah **7:18**), and does so without compromising his holiness. It is to believe in this God, who became flesh, and in whom we find fullness of both grace and truth (John 1:14). Because Jesus—this God—drank the cup of wrath, we can now drink the cup of grace and mercy. The Son of God tells us the truth about ourselves—just as God did so strongly and starkly through Micah—in order that we might appreciate the grace he came to offer, which God points us to through Micah, and indeed throughout the entire Old Testament. We can experience the grace of God because of this one individual who provided the resolution for all of

> How can we hate injustice, be merciful, and forgive those who harm us? There is only one way.

the apparently irreconcilable tension between the holiness and mercy of God. The verdict has been declared. We are free to go. The court is adjourned. We are now free to live our lives for our gracious and holy God, and for the good of others who need our mercy.

Who is a God like him? No one. Whom else would we want to love and live for?

Questions for reflection

1. Do you struggle to accept your brokenness, or to live with boldness (or both!)? What would change if you remembered that you can live with "bold brokenness"?

2. Can you see any ways in which a misunderstanding of how God treats you has caused an unhealthy relationship dynamic with someone close to you? What might change if you begin to repent honestly before God, and appreciate forgiveness from God?

3. How has the book of Micah shaped:
   - your view of who God is?
   - your pursuit of kindness and justice?

GLOSSARY

Agnosticism: the position of being unsure about something, on the basis that there is not enough evidence.

Analogy: a comparison between two things, usually using one of them to explain or clarify the other.

Annals: historical records, e.g. the Old Testament books of 1 and 2 Kings and 1 and 2 Chronicles.

Apologetic: reasoned argument in defense of Christian truth.

Apostate: someone who has abandoned their previous commitment to a religion.

Birthright: in ancient Middle-Eastern cultures, the oldest son inherited the possession (and sometimes position) of his father.

Cast the line by lot: making a decision based on a seemingly random outcome, like the toss of a coin. However, in the Old Testament casting lots with the Urim and Thummim was a God-given way of receiving his guidance.

Christendom: the area of the world where Christianity is either the state religion, or dominates the culture and is subscribed to by the majority of citizens.

Constantine: Roman Emperor from AD306 (though without full control) to AD337, Constantine professed faith in Christ on the eve of the battle that won him the western half of the Roman Empire in 312. Under his rule, Christianity became the favored religion for the first time.

Contusion: an injury to body tissue, usually without any cut.

Covenant: a binding agreement between two parties.

Cultic: a practice or ceremony that is part of following a religious cult.

Curetting: scooping up.

Eastern mysticism: approaches to religious practice based on or inspired by eastern religions such as Buddhism and Hinduism. The hallmark of mysticism is the attempt to commune with God and experience him through practices such as meditation.

Elijah: an Old Testament prophet who announced God's judgment for his people's idolatry.

Endemic: characteristic; widespread.

Exile: referring to the period when the majority of the Jewish population (and all of their surviving elite) were exiled from the land that God had promised their ancestor Abraham, and taken to Babylon, between 586 BC and 538 BC.

Existential: a school of thought which starts with an "existential crisis"—a crushing realization that life is apparently meaningless.

God's economy: the way that God has set up his world.

Grace: unmerited favor. In the Bible, "grace" is usually used to describe how God treats his people. Because God is full of grace, he gives believers eternal life (Ephesians 2:4-8); he also gives them gifts to use to serve his people (Ephesians 4:7, 11-13).

Holistic: complete; concerned with the whole of something rather than a part of it.

Incarnate: the incarnation was the coming of the divine Son of God as a human, in the person of Jesus Christ.

Iniquity: huge injustice; wicked act.

Intrinsically: at the core; belonging to the essence of something.

Invisible hand: the idea that there is an unobservable market force that, in a free market, enables the demand for something and the supply of that thing to match.

Israel: in this context, the northern kingdom in which God's people lived, centered on the capital, Samaria. (The people of Israel divided into two kingdoms during the reign of King Rehoboam, son of King **Solomon**, in around 930 BC).

Jim Crow: racist laws passed by southern states in the United States towards the end of the nineteenth century, which forced black citizens to live separately, barring them from certain places and educational institutions, and from holding particular offices, and making it hard for them to vote. These laws continued to be enforced until 1965.

Judah: in this context, the southern kingdom in which God's people lived, centered on the capital, Jerusalem (see **Israel**).

Justification: the declaration that someone is not guilty, not condemned, completely innocent.

Mediator: someone who brings two enemies together and makes it possible for them to be friends again.

Metaphor: an image which is used to explain something, but which is not to be taken literally (e.g. "The news was a dagger to his heart").

Messianic: having to do with God's promised, universal, eternal King—the Messiah, or Christ.

Moral psychologist: someone who studies the way people discern what is right and wrong, what drives someone's behavior and decisions, etc.

Moralistic: an attitude to life where what matters most (and, in terms of heaven, ultimately and eternally) is how someone behaves.

Moses: the leader of God's people at the time when God brought them out of slavery in Egypt. God communicated his law (including the Ten Commandments) through Moses, and under his leadership guided them toward the land he had promised to give them.

Nihilistic: a view that traditional beliefs are groundless, and that existence is senseless and pointless.

Omniscient: having infinite and perfect understanding.

Oxymoronic: something that is a contradiction, e.g. "a cold heatwave" or "to rush slowly."

Pagan: someone who doesn't know and worship the true God.

Paradoxical: two true statements that seem to be contradictory, but aren't.

Pharisee: leaders of a first-century Jewish sect who were extremely strict about keeping God's laws externally, and who added extra laws around God's law, to ensure that they wouldn't break it.

Plowshares: the blade of a plow; the part that cuts the furrow in the ground.

Power play: a plan or approach to a situation that is calculated to increase a person's power, standing, or influence.

Remnant: a small remaining quantity of something. In the Bible, it refers to the small number of Jews who returned from the exile from the land in Babylon.

Saul: the first king of Israel (see 1 Samuel 8 – 10).

Shalom: peace, harmony, wholeness, completeness, prosperity.

Solomon: the third king of the twelve tribes of Israel—King David's son.

Sovereignly: having supreme authority and complete control.

Steward: in this context, meaning those who are employed by someone to manage their household, estate, and/or affairs.

Subpoena: issued by a court to command someone to appear before that court, and warn them of a penalty if they fail to.

The market: here, meaning the buying and selling of goods, both within a state but also across state borders.

Tithe: here, referring to the Old Testament command to give a tenth of someone's crops.

Transgression: breaking of a law.

Yahweh: the name by which God revealed himself to Moses (Exodus 3:13-14). Literally, it means, "I am who I am" or, "I will be who I will be." Most English-language Bibles translate it as "LORD."

Zion: another name for Jerusalem (more specifically, the mountain upon which it was built).

BIBLIOGRAPHY

■ David & Patricia Alexander, *Eerdmans Handbook to the Bible* (Eerdmans, 1983)

■ Peter Berger, *The Homeless Mind: Modernization and Consciousness* (Vintage, 1974)

■ Andy Crouch, *Playing God* (IVP USA, 2013)

■ Robert Fuller, *All Rise* (Berrett-Koehler, 2006)

■ Jonathan Haidt, *The Happiness Hypothesis: Finding Modern Truth in Ancient Wisdom* (Basic Books, 2006)

■ Cynthia Heimel, *If You Can't Live Without Me, Why Aren't You Dead Yet?!* (Grove, 1991)

■ Emmanuel Katongole & Chris Rice, *Reconciling All Things*, (IVP USA, 2008)

■ Timothy Keller, *Gospel Communication* (unpublished)

■ Timothy Keller, *Counterfeit Gods: The Empty Promises of Money, Sex, and Power, and the Only Hope that Matters* (Penguin, 2011)

■ Timothy Keller, *Judges for You* in the God's Word For You series (The Good Book Company, 2013)

■ Tim Keller, *Kings Cross* (Dutton, 2011)

■ Tim Keller, *The Freedom of Self Forgetfulness: The Path to True Christian Joy* (10Publishing, 2012)

■ Timothy Keller, *Walking With God through Pain and Suffering* (Dutton, 2013)

■ C.S. Lewis, *Letters to Malcolm: Chiefly on Prayer* (Harcourt, 1964)

- Rebecca Manley Pippert, *Hope Has Its Reasons* (IVP USA, 2001)

- David Prior, *The Message of Joel, Micah & Habakkuk* in the Bible Speaks Today series (IVP Academic, 1999)

- Robert Putnam, *Our Kids: The American Dream in Crisis* (Simon & Schuster, 2015)

- Peter Shaffer, *Equus* (Avon, 1974)

- Bruce Waltke, *Micah* in *Obadiah, Jonah and Micah* in the Tyndale Old Testament Commentary series (IVP USA, 2009)

- Edward Welch, *Running Scared* (New Growth Press, 2007)

- Edward Welch, *When People are Big and God is Small* (P&R, 1997)

- Nicholas Wolterstorff, *Hearing the Call: Liturgy, Justice, Church, and the World* (Eerdmans, 2011)

Micah for...
Bible-study Groups

Stephen Um's **Good Book Guide** to Micah is the companion to this resource, helping groups of Christians to explore, discuss and apply the book together. Six studies—each including Investigation, Apply, Getting Personal, Pray, and Explore More sections—take you through the whole prophecy of Micah. Includes a concise Leader's Guide at the back.

Daily Devotionals

Explore daily devotional helps you open up the Scriptures and will encourage and equip you in your walk with God. Available as a quarterly booklet, *Explore* is also available as an app, where you can download Stephen's notes on Micah, alongside contributions from trusted Bible teachers including Timothy Keller, Mark Dever, Tim Chester, Albert Mohler, Jr., and Juan Sanchez.

Find out more at:
www.thegoodbook.com/explore

More For You

Galatians For You

"The book of Galatians is dynamite. It is an explosion of joy and freedom which leaves us enjoying a life of blessing. I pray that it explodes in your heart as you read this book."

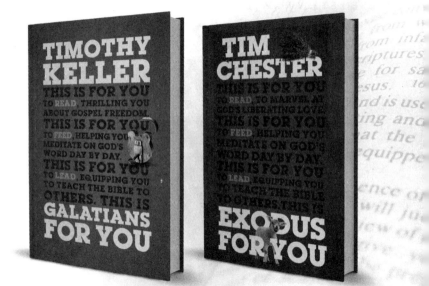

Exodus For You

"Exodus is key to understanding Jesus. It is an exciting story, a historical story and—as it points us to and inspires us to worship Jesus—it is *our* story."

The Whole Series

- **Exodus For You**
  Tim Chester
- **Judges For You**
  Timothy Keller
- **Ruth For You**
  Tony Merida
- **1 Samuel For You**
  Tim Chester
- **2 Samuel For You**
  Tim Chester
- **Psalms For You**
  Christopher Ash
- **Proverbs For You**
  Kathleen Nielson
- **Daniel For You**
  David Helm
- **Micah For You**
  Stephen Um
- **Luke 1-12 For You**
  Mike McKinley
- **Luke 12-24 For You**
  Mike McKinley
- **John 1-12 For You**
  Josh Moody
- **John 13-21 For You**
  Josh Moody
- **Acts 1-12 For You**
  Albert Mohler

- **Acts 13-28 For You**
  Albert Mohler
- **Romans 1-7 For You**
  Timothy Keller
- **Romans 8-16 For You**
  Timothy Keller
- **2 Corinthians For You**
  Gary Millar
- **Galatians For You**
  Timothy Keller
- **Ephesians For You**
  Richard Coekin
- **Philippians For You**
  Steven Lawson
- **Colossians & Philemon For You**
  Mark Meynell
- **1 & 2 Timothy For You**
  Phillip Jensen
- **Titus For You**
  Tim Chester
- **James For You**
  Sam Allberry
- **1 Peter For You**
  Juan Sanchez
- **Revelation For You**
  Tim Chester

Find out more about these resources at:
www.thegoodbook.com/for-you

Good Book Guides
for groups and individuals

Judges: The flawed and the flawless

Timothy Keller
Founding Pastor, Redeemer Presbyterian Church, Manhattan

Welcome to a time when God's people were deeply flawed, often failing, and struggling to live in a world which worshipped other gods. Our world is not so different—we need Judges to equip us to live for God in our day, and remind us that he is a God of patience and mercy.
Also by Tim Keller: Romans 1–7; Romans 8–16; Galatians

Daniel: Staying strong in a hostile world

David Helm
Lead Pastor, Holy Trinity Church, Chicago

The first half of Daniel is well known and much loved. The second is little read and less understood! David Helm leads groups through the whole book, showing how the truths about God in the second half enabled Daniel and his friends—and will inspire us—to live faithful, courageous lives.

Esther: Royal rescue

Jane McNabb
Chair of the London Women's Convention

The experience of God's people in Esther's day helps us in those moments when we question God's sovereignty, his love, or his faithfulness. Their story reveals that despite appearances, God is in control, and he answers his people's prayers—often in most unexpected ways.

1 Corinthians 1–9: Challenging church

Mark Dever
Senior Pastor of Capitol Hill Baptist Church in
Washington DC and President of 9Marks Ministries

The church in Corinth was full of life, and just as full of problems. As you read how Paul challenges these Christians, you'll see how you can contribute to your own church becoming truly shaped by the gospel.
Also by Mark Dever: 1 Corinthians 10–16

James: Genuine faith

Sam Allberry
Speaker, Ravi Zacharias International Ministries

Many Christians long for a deeper, more whole-hearted Christian life. But what does that look like? This deeply practical letter was written to show us, and will reveal how to experience joy in hardships, patience in suffering and whole-heartedness in how you speak, act and pray.
Also by Sam Allberry: Man of God; Biblical Manhood

1 Peter: Living well on the way home

Juan Sanchez
Preaching Pastor, High Pointe Baptist Church, Austin, Texas

The Christian life, lived well, is not easy—because we don't belong in this world. Learn from Peter how to journey on rather than retreat, and to do so with joy and hope, rather than gritted teeth.

BIBLICAL | RELEVANT | ACCESSIBLE

At The Good Book Company, we are dedicated to helping Christians and local churches grow. We believe that God's growth process always starts with hearing clearly what he has said to us through his timeless word—the Bible.

Ever since we opened our doors in 1991, we have been striving to produce Bible-based resources that bring glory to God. We have grown to become an international provider of user-friendly resources to the Christian community, with believers of all backgrounds and denominations using our books, Bible studies, devotionals, evangelistic resources, and DVD-based courses.

We want to equip ordinary Christians to live for Christ day by day, and churches to grow in their knowledge of God, their love for one another, and the effectiveness of their outreach.

Call us for a discussion of your needs or visit one of our local websites for more information on the resources and services we provide.

Your friends at The Good Book Company

thegoodbook.com | thegoodbook.co.uk
thegoodbook.com.au | thegoodbook.co.nz
thegoodbook.co.in